MICROPHONES AND MUDDY BOOTS

MICROPHONES
AND
MUDDY BOOTS

*A Journey into
Natural History Broadcasting*

DEREK JONES
Illustrations by Paul Nicholas

DAVID & CHARLES
Newton Abbot   London   North Pomfret (Vt)

British Library Cataloguing in Publication Data

Jones, Derek *1927–*
   Microphones and muddy boots: a journey into
   natural history broadcasting.
   1. British Broadcasting Corporation
   2. Natural history radio programmes –
   Great Britain
   I. Title
   791.44'5   PN1991.8.N3

   ISBN 0–7153–8918–1

Photoset in Linotron Sabon by
Northern Phototypesetting Co, Bolton
and printed in Great Britain
by A. Wheaton & Co Ltd, Hennock Road, Exeter
for David & Charles Publishers plc
Brunel House Newton Abbot Devon

Published in the United states of America
by David & Charles Inc
North Pomfret Vermont 05053 USA

CONTENTS

This book is dedicated with gratitude to
the many naturalists and producers who made
my broadcasts possible and to the listeners
who encouraged me with their enthusiasm.
May they find pleasure too in my memories.

1
IN THE BEGINNING

Lucky is the man who can sit back and reflect that most of his working life has been spent pursuing his hobby. Natural history has always been my hobby and for more than twenty years it has kept the wolf from the door – although at times its howling has come too close for comfort. It's been a case of going places and meeting people and enjoying new experiences.

Cold and gale-swept promontories, isolated uninhabited islands, draughty hides, caves, moors and woodlands, snow-covered peaks, sun-drenched Mediterranean beaches, and above the Alpine tree-lines: all have beckoned, all have been grist to the natural history broadcasting mill. Indeed, where there is wildlife – even in a kitchen pantry, a compost heap, an old outside lavatory or a raised moorland bog *The Living World* has been there.

It might seem rather outlandish to go bird-watching right

in the West End of London on the roof of Broadcasting House, but in fact it's not a bad place to be: some few feet below the flight-lines yet sufficiently above the roar of London's traffic to make a broadcast possible. Yet on that day, looking desperately for the kestrel that had been nesting in a niche on the front of the Langham opposite, my mind was in another time – the time when the only wings over London had black crosses on them, the Heinkels, Junkers and Dorniers of the Luftwaffe unloading their cargo of destruction on the City.

I had been on that roof then, wearing a steel helmet for protection, sent up there from the Control Room in the bowels of the building down at a level next to the Bakerloo line. For security reasons, the firemen of the building were on the roof during the raids and in their draughty hut was a microphone connected to a loudspeaker in the Control Room. Throughout the raids the watchers kept up a commentary, describing where the last stick of bombs had fallen. It was a graphic picture of events in London, but on this night the microphone suddenly went dead. Two of us were despatched to the roof. We knew there were no casualties as the firemen also had telephonic communication. When we reached the top we found what had been suspected all along: a loose lead on one of the microphone terminals. Indeed, the greatest danger on the roof of that noble building was not so much the German bombs but the shrapnel from the anti-aircraft guns in Hyde Park firing barrages at the bombers. What goes up must come down and some of those pieces could be lethal.

But my lifelong flirtation with natural history broadcasting began earlier than this – a long time before the extraordinary cheerfulness of wartime London – in Taunton, in the depths of the Somerset countryside. Indeed, the family home was even deeper, some miles south of the town and isolated in woodlands with the next habitation a mile and a half away. It was a spot where badgers regularly had runs and were the greatest hazard to those of us on bikes of a dusky evening; where nightingales sang the summer through, kept you awake at night and where once we found a nest, close to the ground in a privet bush.

It was a paradise for someone with nothing more at that time than a passing interest in the wildlife around him, yet here it was cemented. One of the first pieces of serious study came about when I was sent off to the garden to dig a trug of potatoes. Up with the spuds came a large, very brown pupa. Paternal commonsense and a pretty good knowledge of local natural history suggested that as it had come out of the soil why not put it back in the soil, but in captivity – and then wait and see.

The box was a work of art! Soundly constructed, it had a small lid and even the luxury of one section capped with that perforated zinc once used to prevent flies from entering meat safes. Moist soil was placed in the bottom of the box and the large 'lozenge' carefully buried in it. A cellar with windows offered an even temperature for my mystery. Some time later – it could only have been a matter of a few weeks – a squeak was heard in the cellar, like a cornered mouse, coming from the box. I knew enough to know that I could expect a moth, but was concerned on hearing the noise that one of the cellar mice had taken up residence. Carefully opening the lovingly constructed lid, I revealed the moth. What else but that beautiful insect with the symbol of the skull on its back: the death's-head hawk-moth. It was a piece of personal discovery followed by a lesson. I then let the animal go.

My time to go as well, and here was the beginning of the coming together of broadcasting and the animals of the wild. At Taunton there was a small BBC transmitter. A friend had walked this road; a vacancy as a YT (Youth under Training) in the Engineering Division occurred and beckoned.

Taunton was merely an introduction to the ways of BBC engineers. Very soon I was off on a course to London and then to the depths of cider and perry country in Shropshire where we learnt as much of our ability to hold liquor as we did about the laws of impedance and resistance. Trouble was, we couldn't resist the local brew. Those idyllic days, in which the course was beautifully organised into an equal number of the two sexes, came to an end and thirty or so trainees waited for their marching orders. No chance of it being back to Taunton. The piece of paper came not like a buff-coloured OHMS envelope, but rather as a verdict on one's understanding of *Ohm's* law: Jones, D.A., 21379, London Control Room.

Being in the great control centre of BBC broadcasting throughout the world in wartime Britain meant for the newly arrived and supposedly trained engineer being a member, quite literally, of the 'Teddy Bears' Picnic'! This picnic, though, was a recording, a ten-inch HMV record made by Henry Hall and the BBC Dance Orchestra. Its harmonics and the range of the frequencies still haunt me. This record was reckoned to be the most perfect in technical quality so far made and became the official engineering test record. We young engineers stalked the floors of Broadcasting House from the sub-basement to the eighth floor carrying copies of that record with headphones nonchalantly slung around our necks, looking like hospital doctors making their rounds. Perhaps it was a status symbol, but the real job was studio testing. Before every rehearsal in any studio and before any transmission, the technical facilities had to be thoroughly checked: microphones, amplifiers, talk-back, telephones, studio warning lights, plugs in the walls, terminals and the banks of turntables. There could be eight or even ten in some, but more usually four. Every one had to have a dose of the 'Picnic'! – after having a new 'tooth', of course, in the form of a fresh needle.

These tests were carried out over the circuit to the Control Room where another minion checked each of the testing operations, indicating by a signal light when all was well. To ease the tedium of the job, we pretended to be real broadcasters in testing the microphones, competent players of records with 'Picnic'. So much so, that we would carefully set up four copies of the record and go from one turntable to the next with such aplomb that the colleague listening in the Control Room could be fooled that he or she had heard only one record when, on our good days, six turntables had actually been used. It's quite simple really. Get all records on all turntables started at the same moment and you can go from one to the next with no break and no join.

It was during one such operation that a then senior drama producer came up after the performance and suggested that broadcasting was better than playing the fool with Henry Hall and the BBC Dance Orchestra. Another arrow had been fired: another direction sign on the way to the future. But there was not much that could be done about it then, since large sums of money had been expended on making me into a competent engineer and the way out had a door marked very firmly 'closed'.

In a way, it was a blessing that the transition didn't happen there and then for the nerve centre, the Control Room, was probably one of the most exciting places to be, but the lure of the microphone would not be sublimated by sitting at control desks. During night shifts the hectic life eased a pace to allow a rota of meals, a reading of papers, even a quiet game of cards, and there was an empty continuity studio with a plentiful supply of gramophone records – 78s of course. These were boxed and labelled 'fill-up records' and were frequently changed. They were vital in continuity as a fill between programmes in case of a breakdown or an under-run. A wide selection was needed: to be a tasteful bridge between programmes or a fitting fill in a breakdown without inviting odious comparisons. There were therefore boxes of classical records, light music and, my love, swing and jazz. So when all was quiet during those long nights of a twelve-hour shift there would be a 'record programme'. My choice was for the Glen Millers, Benny

11

Goodmans and Quintets of the Hot Club of France; others would go for the Bachs and Beethovens – this, of course, when no raid kept us on our toes. These impromptu programmes were relayed to other BBC stations up and down the country. (Have you noticed that my initials are also an indication of the way life was opening up before me?)

Practical jokes were part of the stock in trade. On each shift one engineer, male or female, sat at a desk outside the office of the Senior Control Room Engineer taking service messages. These were sometimes merely informative, but were occasionally urgent from the outlying centres. One came in from the Engineer-in-Charge at Daventry – urgent. 'Aerial array collapsed. Please send skyhooks.' The message was thrust into the hands of the man in the inner sanctum. He must have had a sense of humour for nothing more was heard about it except the young lady who received the message was perhaps a little wiser about how transmitter aerials are suspended. This prank was made possible because every line coming into the Control Room could be picked up on terminal bays in the back of the nerve centre before they appeared on telephone bays. It was possible to plug in a portable telephone where you couldn't be seen, and I think the whole thing was forgotten because 'Sir' realised that his young bloods were finding their way around and that was vitally important; in some circumstances it could have been critical.

The carpet did await me once, and it was a bit of a roasting. From a studio in the depths of the building the Queen of The Netherlands was making a broadcast to her loyal subjects in occupied Holland. With any royal broadcast the top engineering brass was heavily evident. There was also a bit of a flap on the bay responsible for the distribution of world reports to recording channels all over London. To identify that one had the correct line to the right channel, a burst of line-up tone would be sent before the recording deadline. I was conscious of the royal broadcast coming over the loudspeaker in the room behind me. It came to an end and the strains of the national anthem of The Netherlands struck up a patriotic note. At that moment there was a plug in my hand to send some of that line-up tone to Bush House. Plug into hole. Line-up tone coming out of the loudspeaker as well as the national anthem. Pulled out plug, tone disappeared. The carpeting was quite mild, and I suppose it is a claim to fame to have marred a royal broadcast! But implication during those wartime days was serious enough, for that interruption to the anthem could have been a secret message to underground patriots and, even though it wasn't, it might have been construed as such by German intelligence.

These were exciting days: the excitement of being at the hub of wartime broadcasting tempered by the horrors of the bombing, the death, the destruction. It was nothing like as bad as the early days. We experienced little more than nuisance raids, and our defences were such that fewer and fewer bombers of the Luftwaffe were penetrating to Central London. There was always a slight apprehension, though, on blinking into the daylight of Regent Street after a night shift in the artificial light to look around and see if familiar landmarks still stood. And would the cosy lodgings in Wembley be there intact? They always were, but there were one or two near misses.

Such was the pattern of the shift rota in dear old Broadcasting House with a sixteen-day sequence that, after the final four nights on duty, came freedom for very nearly five days before returning for the evening shift. It was a chance to get away to the house in the woods, back to see if the aggressive cob still defended the nearby pond, back to what in wartime days was something of a false life – no queues here. If there was meat rationing it wasn't really noticed since a brace of rabbits could be had for the pot simply by setting snares; vegetables could be had in plenty from the garden, fruit from the orchard, watercress from a fresh spring overflow, nuts from the trees in the wild woods and in the autumn blackberries as big and luscious as you've ever seen. And who would not be welcome back in 'the Smoke' at the end of that four-day break carrying a brace of rabbits?

Broadcasting with the voice was still some distance away but broadcasting in code was next. Mysterious enquiries were made among the staff: 'Has anyone operated a Morse key? Does anyone know the Morse code?' There is a piece of advice in service circles about never volunteering for anything. In this case the mystery was so intriguing that I confessed to being a member of the Air Training Corps, and to being familiar with the code as well as the key.

Familiarity with the dots and dashes, and the touch of an apprentice midwife on the key, were very quickly pushed from a nodding acquaintance into something nearing competence. But no one would explain the unseemly rush. Then a mysterious corner of the balcony above the Control Room was boxed off. Equipment was hastily installed: a transmitter, a short-wave receiver. Mic Charlie Mic was a going concern. It soon became clear why this was all so hush-hush and what part MCM was to play in the next few months.

The build-up for D-Day was under way: the invasion of Hitler's Atlantic wall-enclosed Europe. The Allies were massing for Operation Overlord and the penny dropped conclusively that the invasion was imminent when we carried out test transmissions with another BBC transmitter 'somewhere on the south coast', the BBC transmitter that was to land after the invasion foothold had been made and then provide BBC, American and Canadian correspondents with access to their respective networks. War reporting, on the spot, was flapping its fledgling wings.

The story of the War Report Unit is well documented elsewhere (*BBC War Report*, published by the Oxford University Press), but suffice it to say within two weeks of D-day the first BBC mobile transmitter, MCO – Mic Charlie Oboe – was on in Normandy. Those days were the most exciting of all. One was at the very centre of the war, hearing it all happening long before it went on the air to listeners to the Home Service or the General Forces Programme or the BBC Service around the world – long before our American and Canadian allies heard the news. It was all around me! And I was a small cog with a Morse key in my hand, one of a team, chain-smoking the nerves at bay, helping to mould this revolution in broadcasting. Security was high. That is the reason why we had to operate the wrist-aching Morse key while Mic Charlie Oboe came up in plain speech. Had there been a microphone in that shack in Broadcasting House and should a bomb or in those days a doodlebug or V2 be dropped within spitting distance, then the explosion would have been heard over the air and undoubtedly picked up by enemy intelligence. Yet one could, with discretion, let the little word drop. The wife of a BBC war correspondent worked in the same West End office as the daughter of my landlady. There was never a direct message: just 'We've heard from him today – he's all right.' No questions or favours asked, none given. Just wartime comradeship, within the bounds of the Official Secrets Act.

Breaching the Atlantic wall was the beginning. Eventually came the break-out and the advance across France, into the Low Countries. The original BBC mobile transmitter, MCO, was joined by two sisters, MCN and MCP. Our traffic through London and MCM grew and grew, especially when American transmitters joined in, and at peak American network time there was a queue of American reporters waiting to go 'live' into their respective networks. They were brave men in broadcasting terms. Going live with no word cue that they could hear. They had to rely on split-second timing and a stopwatch. It was nothing to them to start a report at, for instance, 13.02.45 (two minutes forty-five seconds past one o'clock) and talk for precisely one minute and ten seconds. So that little shack on the Control Room balcony was a busy place and an exciting place as the reports from the BBC correspondents in the various sectors plied the War Reporting Unit with their material: some of it already recorded out in the field on the ingenious portable disc recorders, others the straight report from the mobile transmitter. People like Frank Gillard, Wynford Vaughan Thomas, Guy Byam, Chester Wilmot, Pierre Lefevre, Robert Barr and more made a mark on the history of broadcasting.

Another significant landmark happened shortly after: the General Forces Programme became the Allied Expeditionary Forces Programme and this is the point when the BBC put off the Reithian dinner jacket and became less formal – it had to. Here were broadcasters from three nations: two North American, one British. The Americans and Canadians were what we would describe as 'laid back'; they were not scriptbound, but informal and friendly. The British had to join them. They patently couldn't beat them. Perhaps a few of our traits and concerns rubbed off on them. Provided informality is combined with accuracy, then the formula looks good. And it was. What talent it had to call on: Glen Miller and the American Band of the AEF (by any other name the Glen Miller Orchestra); the British Band of the AEF with George Melachrino and sub-sections of them. Variety programmes from the United States provided by the Armed Forces Radio Service on great LP discs from Bob Hope and all the great Hollywood entertainers, and the expertise of the American Forces Network, AFN.

So much happened in those days: my duties seemed to be split between the technical side of the AEF Programme and that cosy corner on the balcony. Two reports that came through stand out because, unknown at the time, they pointed towards the future. One was the signing of the surrender document on Luneburg Heath by Monty with what remained of the German High Command in a typical Monty 'no nonsense' piece of stage management. Hearing that, before it went on the air to BBC listeners, made one feel humble – and thankful that it was all over. The other was from Hamburg. A little wartime light relief had come by listening to a man who was a caricature of himself, a man whose real name was William Joyce. He was better known as Lord Haw-Haw, a tool of the German propaganda machine. His broadcasts from Hamburg always began with the words, 'Germany calling, Germany calling' and his news broadcasts were designed to undermine our morale by describing for instance, where German bombs had fallen the previous night, by delivering tirades against Churchill, the government and the alliance and giving predictions on the outcome of the war. I'm not sure whether his last talk ever went on the air, but I've certainly heard tapes of it when the once haughty Haw-Haw had patently taken more than a little Dutch courage to see him through. But when Wynford Vaughan Thomas broadcast from the studio used by the un-belted Lord, the war was to all intents and purposes over. And for me another phase was drawing to a close. Within a few weeks, sunk deep in a small BBC personal file was the number 21379; instead, 14088425.

You know what it is, but you don't want to pick it up. Eventually, the buff envelope fell like a stage whisper onto the doormat, requiring my services elsewhere: Maidstone, initially, to be square-bashed into shape. It took all of a year to achieve, six months intensive infantry training, wearing the familiar Jellalabad badge of the Somerset Light Infantry, skirting a War Office Selection Board, transferring to the Royal Electrical & Mechanical Engineers, being put through a nine-month course telescoped into six weeks to become an instructor and incurring the wrath of the REME Commanding Officer when he found on his desk a War Office posting for one of his three lecturers designate: 14088425 Private Jones, D.A., to be embarked for Hamburg and the British Forces Network.

Embarkation leave allowed me a final loving look at those Somerset hills and woods, another draught of cider from the farmhouse kitchen of Farmer Shattock at Orchard Portman, and a sight of the spotted flycatchers which had once again nested in the funnel of the downpipe outside my bedroom window. This was it.

The deviousness of a man wanting to get to a particular place at a certain time is really the guile of man the hunter. To be able to circumvent the War Office was no mean achievement but suffice it to say that knowing people in the right places and a word in the right ear can sometimes move mountains. I certainly wrote no letter. The request for that unpopular posting came from Germany. There I found, rather like the irate REME C.O., that people were due for demob and the shortage was not of engineers, but broadcasters. Was there yet again a puppet-master pulling strings behind the scenes? This was a case of being thrown in at the deep end of broadcasting after tip-toeing off the lowest board in a programme that needed an American voice.

If ever there were a University of Broadcasting it was the Forces Broadcasting Service spread around the world. It hived off people uncomfortably clad in khaki, or Navy and RAF blue, into the web of communication: people from show business and radio who could make a greater contribution than being pen-pushing cipher clerks, cooks or corporals of horse. If ever there was a military shambles, it was BFN in Hamburg. The expertise lay not on the parade ground but in the studio, a splendid building standing undamaged like a solitary green elm amid a forest of devastated diseased trees: the Musikhalle, the Concert Hall of the City of Hamburg.

It was a vibrant going concern but one look at the staff and my RSM at the Infantry Training Battalion would have committed the ultimate crime in his book and fainted on the parade ground. Mind you, he was a Coldstream Guardsman. Here were men from every branch of the service: Navy, Army, Air Force, all mixed up with ranks ranging from colonel down to the lowest of the low. But shining through it all was the cameraderie of broadcasting and everyone was on christian name terms. Can you imagine a military unit where a vote was taken during the day on where to *dine* that evening? Should it be the officers' club or the WO's & JO's? If the decision came down on the warrant officers' and sergeants' club, then it meant rustling around for spare uniforms so that the officers could enter the non-commissioned officers' domain. On another night, the reverse decisions had to be made. Then again there was the Control Commission club in which case we all found civilian clothes. How no one was ever picked up by the Military Police I shall never know. Sergeants wearing the pips of a captain, a captain wearing sergeant's stripes? But then, that's broadcasting: the job and the love of it transcended military precedence.

We must have become more than somewhat out of hand when a company sergeant major from the Devons was posted to BFN to instil discipline into the unit. His first idea was that service boots would be worn at all times. And they were – for all of twenty-four hours. It's surprising how much noise a pair of army boots, heavily studded, can make across a studio floor when the wearer exerts a little more than tiptoe pressure! The order was rescinded. But he had another weakness which hammered in the final nail and made him one of the boys. His drinking habits demanded that before breakfast he needed a 'hair of the dog', a pint of frothy German beer served with due respect by the mess waiter. One morning it had somehow taken on an added effervescence produced by a liberal dose of Epsom salts. From that moment military discipline was conveniently forgotten – he went through the motions of doing his job, we got on with ours!

It wasn't difficult; it was fun and if it hadn't been, the staff would never have put in the hours they did. Entertainment was the watchword with very little more than a touching of the forelock towards information or education. There was a noticeboard of the films being shown at the cinemas, and visiting shows and bands performed at the Combined Services Entertainment Unit Theatres, but there was precious little else. But with a war behind them, the forces and the civilians working out there didn't really ask for anything else. The environment was pretty grim and it needed laughs, nostalgia for home and bright lights to keep up morale. The black market flourished, and among troops liberally supplied with cigarettes non-smokers or those with access to extra rations could buy themselves the finest Leica camera or the best Swiss watch for not much more than a song. The value of the cigarette must have been brought home to everyone in those early days after hostilities when, walking along smoking a cigarette, one would be conscious of footsteps behind. It was nothing for several Germans to squabble over the discarded dog-end. All this we could see. We were conscious too of the tremendous efforts very soon made at rebuilding from the ruins of war. Housing projects were non-stop. Once the economy began to shake off the effects of war and the black market, the energy of the nation became apparent – yet such events were not reported on BFN. There was a short daily news bulletin provided by the Control Commission, but very little about the country we occupied. The status quo of war remained: the victor and the vanquished. In retrospect it's easy to be wise, but I think we should have paid more attention to the small part of the world around us.

The informality born of the Allied Expeditionary Forces Programme was continued and extended within the beautiful Musikhalle, where the revolving statue of Brahms looked down with no apparent distaste of the music being dispensed around him. Mind you, he had his moments. Every sunday afternoon there was a 'live' broadcast from the main concert hall which was also relayed by the German network, NWDR. Sitting in continuity one day, the information came from the studio that the concert couldn't start on time as the conductor, Hans Schmidt-Isserstedt, had forgotten the concert scores and was rushing out to get them. This meant a record fill with appropriate music until the great conductor returned. Looking out of the studio window after a ten-minute delay, I saw his car rushing up the street. 'We should soon be able to start today's concert as I've just seen the conductor's car coming towards Broadcasting House.' There was at least a shadow of Reith still hanging around. And for flippancy, there was a hard word or two from the Station Director, a dour Scot, Alec Sutherland, seconded to look after this motley crew by the BBC.

Six very happy years in Hamburg broadcasting on any topic you care to mention (*apart* from Natural History!) was the grounding that any budding microphone-man today would dream about but never be able to achieve. Disc jockey programmes, news reading (those tiddly Control Commission bulletins), continuity work, sports commentaries and running a department. On second thoughts, isn't that just what local radio people are supposed to do? Perhaps after all their roots are back in the ruins of Hamburg for so many of us left there and found a niche with Auntie.

A couple of hair-raising moments I pass on to outside broadcast producers of today. We took on the task of covering the German Motor Racing Grand Prix which had never had an English commentary until the day BFN descended on the Nurburgring in southern Bavaria – a motor-racing circuit nothing like it is today. It was one of Hitler's masterpieces. The lap of the circuit covered just over fourteen miles. We had three commentary points approximately equally placed around the Eifel Mountains, but just consider that the lap speeds in those days on a tortuous circuit were something like 78mph. So when the cars left the starting grid we couldn't expect them back to the line again for ten minutes! The commentators were therefore stretched until the race spread out. My colleague, Hedley Chambers, joined me for this first-time broadcast and to fill in at our third commentary point we threw in a man who knew motor racing, but not broadcasting, the then sports editor of *Autocar*, Gordon Wilkins.

It was in the supporting 500cc race that a youthful Stirling Moss was driving a Kieft, a splendid little car and faster than the Coopers using the same Norton double-knocker engine. The Kieft sported drum brakes at the front end but at the rear, apparently nothing. The secret was a single disc brake mounted inboard and out of sight under the cowelling. Moss put in a couple of very fast practice laps and father Alfred hastened to put the car back out of sight in the transporter. But not before a couple of German correspondents had spotted this car with no brakes on the rear wheels. 'But how, Herr Moss, do you make the car stop?' Stirling came out with the classic riposte 'Who wants to make the so-and-so thing stop?' The Kieft was pushed into the transporter with no more questions.

One other outside broadcast presented problems. Rhine Army HQ put in a request for publicity for the Services Leave Centre at Ehrwald in the Austrian Tyrol. Raymond Baxter and I set forth. High in the mountains, the splendid ski-resort was best approached by the electric railway which climbed its way higher and higher alongside the telephone lines that were to carry our programmes out of Austria and back to Hamburg. During tests there was high interference on the lines and for a time the broadcasts seemed in doubt. Came the day, or days, for several programmes to put the Leave Centre on the map and all was mysteriously well – no interference, clear signals. We discovered afterwards that the Austrian telephone engineer had tracked down the interference to the running of the mountain railway and so he ordered that the trains should stop running during our programmes!

14088425 had by now disappeared. Most of the BFN personnel were now civilians, but my destination was hospital, twelve months out of action and then to knock on the BBC door. 'There's no work, I'm afraid', said Frank Gillard, then Controller in Bristol. Work started two days later!

2
GOOD MORNING

There comes a time in every man's life when he reflects on
what he has achieved and takes the thought a stage further
and ponders on how he will be remembered. So it was one
evening on a train from Bristol Temple Meads to Plymouth
as Alan Gibson and myself sat in the restaurant car and
began, as chaps do after the third glass, to think on our lives
and whether what we regarded as our important
contributions would feature in our obituaries. In Alan's
case, here was a brilliant historian, a highly respected
cricket commentator, a nearly successful parliamentary
candidate for the Liberal party, and man of many parts. As
for myself: modesty forbids that my inner secrets should
here be revealed. But no, as the train drew into Taunton, we
came to the dreadful conclusion that if we were to be
remembered it would be for a programme that in our
opinion was of no great social significance, but we were
lumbered: our contribution to society would be, whether

we liked it or not, *Good Morning*.

The intention of the hierarchy, and Desmond Hawkins in particular (Head of West Regional Programmes in those days) was that this should be a piece of real public service broadcasting to keep people informed about what was going on in the region and at the same time link up Plymouth with its senior BBC sister studios in Bristol: information sprinkled with listeners' request records. We were invited to present it each saturday morning between 8.15 and 9.00am, Alan in Plymouth and me in Bristol and both of us given the freedom, almost unheard of in those days, of having no script! This was dangerous ground not to be trodden lightly, and there must often have been second thoughts in the front office about letting loose two men of widely differing backgrounds likely to set off a radio landmine! Well they may have worried, for even the first programme never reached the expected brief. Even the requests became secondary: the seal was set on that when someone asked to hear a heavy piece of Handel and one of us said, 'Sorry, but here is a splendid song by Ruby Murray.' It must have been Alan. He had a thing about Miss Murray at the time.

Not only was there no script, there was no rehearsal. We used to reach our respective studios half an hour before going on the air, and even then one or other of us would often be late for that first contact call. All we had to do, though, was decide on an order of play for the records we had selected from the week's batch of requests, and we were soon getting two or three hundred requests a week from which we might, on good days, get through seven or eight. But as for any idea of chatting over what we might be talking about during the forty-five minute transmission – never!

With the two of us ad libbing our way through the programme, the studio managers faced a tremendous problem, as they had to play the records on cue. Cue! That was a laugh. It became our habit to make the introductions to those discs as oblique as possible so that the studio managers had to *sense* when we expected any record to be played. Full marks to them all for it wasn't often that the gaps showed and a catch phrase was born to applaud their dexterity. That phrase was 'manual dexterity', meaning that our obscure introductions had been anticipated and the record played where we wanted it. Our technical friends entered into the spirit of the saturday mornings and it was, of course, a matter of pride to them that their performance with the discs should be as professional as possible. Perhaps we talked of 'manual dexterity' too much for sure enough one morning they got their own back and we were to hear a short tape made by two of them featuring a strange Spanish gentleman named Manuel Dexterity! Manuel stayed around for a long time thanks to Barry Paine, one of the studio managers, who was in later years to become a colleague on natural history programmes.

No one was safe. The continuity announcer, Ronnie Short, who always made the introductory announcement to the programme, was very early a target. So was the late Brian Patten, the producer, who became famous as 'Sir' although the spelling was more usually 'cur'. Alan's secretary likewise was affectionately 'Cor'. It all sounds silly in retrospect but it was fun at the time and there hadn't really been anything like it on the radio before, certainly not on the West of England Home Service.

Although our interests were wide apart, Alan and I did have common ground. That was cricket and perhaps it's one of the reasons the programmes worked. During the summer months we concentrated on cricket, and the county players, or perhaps it would be more correct to say Somerset, were the butt for our humour. That we should have shown bias towards Somerset was not intentional, but that a programme such as ours should produce a bitter reaction from Gloucestershire came as a surprise. The broadside came during one of the traditional matches between the two sides at the County Ground at Taunton.

During a bit of a shindig after the first day's play at the County Hotel, Taunton, Alan and I were buttonholed by the then Gloucestershire captain, the short, pugnacious George Emmett. He pointed out in no uncertain terms that we broadcasters on saturday mornings didn't regard Gloucestershire as being part of the Westcountry. We didn't even know he had heard the programme!

This was during the period when Somerset County Cricket Club was known as the United Nations because of the number of overseas players who contributed enormously to what many people regard as one of the most exciting sides of all time. Two who played no small part in the success were Australians, one a former Test player for his country, and the other who should have represented his country, Colin McCool and Bill Alley. They were both extremely likeable men, down to earth, laconic and good company. Needless to say, they very soon became part of the *Good Morning badinage* and gave the occasional interview. Neither was in the first flush of youth, and to differentiate between them in our chats Bill became known as the 'ebullient Australian'. We were very kind since it would not have been out of place to dub him the *old* ebullient Australian. There was always a question mark over his age but, going by the record books, some of which also have doubts, it is reckoned he was forty-two. That year he entered the Somerset record books by scoring ten centuries and three thousand runs in the season. Not content with that, he took a hundred wickets the following year on top of nearly two thousand runs.

The stories that surround him are legion but the one I like best concerns a bowling feat – or rather the wicket he didn't take. On this day, with the right atmosphere and a bit of green on the top of the strip, his deceptively paced bowling was nearly unplayable. So it was when facing Alley that the Reverend David Sheppard as he was then, playing of course for Sussex, found the elusive Alley W. E. at his most dangerous. Six balls in the over came down the pitch and each of them had David playing and missing. At the end of the over an exasperated Alley stood half way down the pitch, hands on hips and eyes raised to the heavens. The gist of what he said is 'How can I have a hope of getting you when you've got Him on your side.' It's supposed to be true. Of Col McCool I can vouch for one of his classics. When asked what he was going to do on retirement he said, in effect, 'I'm going back home, plant some pineapples and sit back and watch the buggers grow.' Great men, great times.

Both cricketers were magnets that attracted youthful autograph hunters. One day, I joined Alan on the County Ground at Taunton for a chat, and at the end of his commentary period at lunchtime we came down the steps from the BBC box in the old pavilion to be buttonholed by a bunch of lads with autograph books in hand asking us politely to sign. Suitably flattered, we signed with the flourish of the self-important. With thanks on both sides (personalities should *always* thank autograph hunters), we started to make steps towards that spot where most men retire during the luncheon interval only to hear one of the hunters saying in less than a stage whisper 'Who are *they* then?' Total deflation – and, in the fickle broadcasting business, no bad thing.

Places, as well as people, were a source for our humour from such unlikely parts as Camborne in Cornwall and Highbridge in Somerset, the tenuous connection between the two being clocks. A listener reported that the four faces of the Camborne clock showed different times and so it became known as the 'Four-faced Liar' closely followed by a similar report on the Highbridge timepiece which had problems with its three faces. Our ribbing may have rubbed off onto the typewriter of a local reporter for we were sent a newspaper cutting of the proceedings of the local council where unfortunately, in a piece of printer's pie, the Town Clerk became in the newspaper report the Town Clock. That ensured his place in the annals of the programme for years, especially as the timepiece suffered the indignity of being demolished in a road accident. It stood at a tricky junction alongside the A38. No more town clock! We received a 'phone call from a lorry driver admitting it was his vehicle that had done the dastardly deed. Another faithful listener!

Then there was Blandford Forumio – sorry, Blandford Forum, that delightful old market town in Dorset. The 'Forumio' came about because there used to be a signpost ten miles from the town where the name and the distance figures were so close that the first glance made it Blandford Forumio. Why it entered our banter is a bit obscure, but there was one night when a milk train going west happened to stop and my colleague hitched a lift to Plymouth. Certainly this station on the old Somerset & Dorset line (known variously as the Slow & Dirty or the Slow & Doubtful) was lamentably short of trains. Indeed, to prove the point on a certain saturday morning my end of *Good Morning* was presented standing on the lines in Blandford Forum station. No trains! We had full co-operation from the station staff and particularly the station master who insisted I return the compliment by crowning their Carnival Queen!

Another town had an alias: Aggie on Horseback. Now it takes a shrewd publicity officer to turn adversity to advantage and for Weston-super-Mare it was a north countryman, Ted Turner. He courted *Good Morning*, or any BBC programme for that matter, with ardent fervour. The resort he promoted could always find its name in the headlines. 'Roses bloom at Christmas in Weston' was his claim, and sure enough he found a few blooms to prove his claim. His beauty contests had as many column inches as 'Miss World' in later years. And as for the balmy climate, forget the weather forecasts, bunions and wet seaweed were his barometers. But to explain the place's strange pseudonym: historians will know that the Royal Sailors' Rests were founded by Dame Agnes Weston and became affectionately known on the mess decks as Aggie Westons.

Hence Weston-super-Mare was Aggie on Horseback.

This is the pride before the fall. Listeners entered into our conversations by providing the ammunition. A competitive spirit entered the convivial battle area. It only needed one new topic raised by one or other of us for a listener somewhere between Brighton and Land's End to cap it. Fly stories were a case in point. The beginning was harmless enough. There were these two flies playing football in a saucer. One said to the other 'We'll have to play better than this next week when we're playing in the cup.' They were corny and harmless, but they came to an end with the help of one of our listeners. As one fly said to the other 'Woe is me for I am undone.' We were taken off the air for three weeks for that one! Would it happen today? It was mild by the standards of the eighties – not only mild, not even worth telling, but in those days it was beyond the pale and banished we were for three weeks of saturday unemployment by the then Head of Programmes in Bristol, Patrick Beech. (And as for those ghastly elephant jokes – we started those too, despite what DJs in later years may claim.)

And then there was one saturday morning when continuity made the ear-catching announcement that Alan and Derek were on their way to Hollywood to receive a top DJ award and listeners would be joining them on board their aircraft in mid-Atlantic. Listeners heard the gentle hum of the aircraft engines in the background; Alan and I chatting about the joys of going to the States for an accolade interrupted by a stewardess enquiring into our every need. We introduced the records and enthused over the flight, while the stewardess came in to offer us more smoked salmon, more champagne and if there was anything else we needed please press the service button. We hadn't touched down on American soil before the broadcast came to an end; nor did we ever make landfall in the USA. This saturday fell on 1 April and the stewardess who made the whole thing so authentic was the beautiful Old Vic actress and my friend for many years, June Barrie. She ad libbed her heart out and, of course, it was easy to play in effects in the background of the engine noise and to distort our voices slightly to simulate a broadcast coming from an aircraft half way across the Atlantic!

That April Fool's gag succeeded like the famous *Panorama* spoof perpetrated by Richard Dimbleby with the spaghetti trees. As Brian Patten, our producer, and I approached the reception desk to leave the building that day the commissionaire thrust a 'phone into my hand. It was from Bob Forbes, newspaper reporter and broadcaster. 'Derek Jones.' There was a moment's pause before Bob's voice came back: 'You sod, you're really in Bristol and not on that so and so aeroplane.' He then confessed he had been taken in by the broadcast and had filed a story of our Hollywood award to the *Daily Mirror*. He cancelled it pretty sharply. Brian had a 'phone call too. From Frank Gillard, then Controller of the BBC West Region, complaining that he hadn't been told of the honour that was coming the way of two of his broadcasters!

Ah well, we had eleven years of beer money, meeting many, many people, being something of a cult and enjoying ourselves. It wasn't until more than twenty years later that I realised what *Good Morning* had meant to our listeners when I was severely taken to task by a chap because we hadn't played his request on his wedding day in 1963. He still harbours the grudge. The other side of the coin is somewhat humbling. A solicitor's letter reached me recently from a firm in Plymouth. A lady in the city had remembered Alan and me in her will and left us a small sum each as a token of her appreciation of the programme *Good Morning*.

PAUL NICHOLLS

3
COMMENTATORS ARE VULNERABLE

It was thought a good idea at the time to take Acker Bilk and his jazz band to a remote part of Somerset on New Year's Eve to take part in a nationwide programme called *Dancing in the New Year* where the action moved around the country in a musical kaleidoscope reflecting on its journey differing musical tastes and contrasting atmospheres. Acker and our production team went to a club room in the old market town of Dunster in the shadow of the castle. We weren't due to go on the air until sometime between 11pm and midnight and there was the pub bar downstairs where we could all keep out the winter chills and generally get in the mood. What we didn't know was that the landlord had a goodly supply, at a very cheap price, of a wine much liked by the Paramount Jazz Band. They enjoyed it, as did the landlord who counted his blessings at having a clientele who spent so lavishly.

The broadcast was carefully planned. We should be on the air for about ten minutes and listeners would join us with Acker just reaching the end of a jazzy offering. He would then play three other numbers, which I should introduce and at the end of the last one hand on to the next stop in this round-the-country jaunt. It was a simple formula and foolproof, but we hadn't taken into account the wine. Sure enough, listeners joined us in Dunster with Acker and the band blowing their hearts out. Ten minutes later they were still ad libbing their way through the selfsame melody and my only chore was to shout a greeting just after our part of the programme began and shout a farewell combined with good wishes for the New Year about nine minutes later. The band played beautifully and the error of their ways was probably not even noticed by the listeners.

My good friend Acker figured prominently in another broadcast which he and I and many more would rather forget: the fifth Beaulieu Jazz Festival, August Bank Holiday weekend, 1960. It became known later as the Battle of Beaulieu and as one intimately involved who could argue with the description? It had all the makings of a great jazz evening that saturday, a live television transmission with Johnny Dankworth, Acker Bilk, Tubby Hayes, Ronnie Scott, Humphrey Lyttleton and more, and the organisers expected an audience of ten thousand people. What the television audience was, who can tell. Lord Montagu was very much in the public eye at that time and members of the press were there in some number. The setting was perfect: the lawns, Palace House, and a giant fairground merry-go-round as the stage, set against a background of the trees and waters of Beaulieu. Besides which, the weather was kind: it was a balmy evening.

My vantage point, if such it was, was at the side of the merry-go-round stage, with the canvas roof above, and right alongside the twenty to thirty feet of scaffolding erected to carry the lighting needed for the television broadcast. During the evening it became very obvious that Acker's fans had arrived too. They were easily spotted by the gallon jars of cider they carried. Perhaps it's unfair to Acker to say they were 'fans': more likely a great number of them were hooligans doing what hooligans do today with even greater damage to other people's property and themselves. But, undoubtedly, it was Mr Bilk they wanted to hear as their incessant chanting of 'We want Acker' echoing around the Palace House grounds indicated.

The real trouble began as we were on the air. Some people had already climbed the scaffolding to get a better view. Acker came on stage and that was the signal for even louder tribal cries and bedlam. It's not a happy situation for a commentator, huddled by his monitor screen, to glance up and see bodies crawling around the supports of the canvas roofing or to realise that the scaffolding carrying the lighting was definitely swaying and it certainly wasn't a breeze that was making the movement.

During outside broadcasts the commentator hears via an earpiece the words of the producer, in this case Peter Bale. His is the guiding voice while the director selects the shots from the cameras – all calm and ordered even as disorder broke out around us. More and more people invaded the stage; the scaffolding was now festooned with chanting fans waving bottles. Bottles were thrown, the stage invaded, BBC microphones grabbed from the stage. But we were still on the air and at this point Peter Bale's voice came to my ears, unflustered, still at the helm. 'You're on your own Derek – your mic we'll keep live'. In other words, when I saw shots on my monitor that needed explanation I could talk.

The broadcast carried on long after the scheduled time, despite all the problems, until the inevitable happened and the scaffolding gave in to the unequal struggle of bodies and came crashing to the ground, right by my side. Acker left the stage and eventually order was restored. It was a television broadcast of the instant news value that we take for granted today, but in those days – over twenty-five years ago – it was a sensation. As it occurred late at night the press couldn't make the deadlines for the sunday papers, except for the *News of the World*. Their final edition carried the Battle of Beaulieu across the front page. (That is the *only* time my name has appeared in that particular paper!)

I must take Lord Montagu to task for one remark he makes in his book *The Gilt and the Gingerbread* (published by Michael Joseph). In his comments on the Jazz Festival and the riot he writes, 'Derek Jones, the BBC Commentator, for once was lost for words.' The words were certainly there but perhaps some people couldn't hear them in the fracas.

Commentators always have to find words but they are only as good as their homework! Horse-racing commentators, particularly Peter O'Sullevan, are probably the best. They have to spot, often in difficult visibility, the colours of the racing silks and put instant names to both horse and jockey. There is a danger, of course, of doing too much research and being concerned to get every ounce out of it to the detriment of the commentary. 'And this is Lauda in his Marlborough Maclaren, past world champion, the man who retired from Grand Prix racing at the Canadian Grand Prix to concentrate on his airline business and then made a dramatic comeback now making a bid to win his own, the Austrian Grand Prix.' By which time not only has Lauda disappeared from the television screen but seven other cars have gone through with positions changing and some poor driver belting the Armco barrier to the detriment of both his car and himself. Motor-racing commentators have a difficult task, often in foreign countries where the directors of the outside broadcasts may not be as competent as those of the BBC. But the rule remains: talk only of the picture you and the viewers are seeing at that moment. The trivia you've got up your sleeve may be used in slack times.

There's never any lack of background material for royal occasions. The press-pack sent to all commentators and journalists is a thick tome with every conceivable piece of information you need – and more besides. There was one occasion when the Queen and the Duke of Edinburgh were making a visit to Plymouth in the Royal Yacht *Britannia*. Timetables for such events are known long in advance, and Alan Gibson and myself were to cover the event for radio on the West of England Home Service. Nowadays, it is accepted that in the sound commentary box there is the facility of a television monitor. During a radio Test Match commentary such phrases as 'Watching that on replay shows it was well wide of third slip and wasn't a chance' are common enough and show the co-operation that now exists between sound and television. On that day, when the royal party came to Plymouth, there was no such aid – Alan and I were on our own. And the royal visitors were behind schedule!

We had done our homework and the Buckingham Palace press-pack and all the information from the Public Relations Department of the City Council were wonderful. We couldn't have asked for more. But more, in the event, would have been useful. Twenty minutes behind schedule, the cavalcade came into our view in the Civic Centre and not a moment too soon. When commentators have to resort to describing the colour of the hats worn by the ladies within their view it's a sure sign that desperation is creeping in and on that royal day in Plymouth we were very near to desperation.

Another day that went down in history was 8 September 1966. Until then, those of us who had to make a journey from the Westcountry to South Wales had either to queue for the antiquated ferry at Aust or else make the long and tedious journey around Gloucester. September 1966 saw the end of all that frustration when the Severn Bridge was opened by Her Majesty the Queen. Wynford Vaughan Thomas on the Welsh side of the water and myself on the English side were the commentators for radio and here was a day when we had the back-up of television monitors so we didn't have to be near the action! Indeed, it was vital to have the television screen since my vantage point was on the left-hand side of the road just short of the cliff drop into the Severn – with a splendid view of the great pillars that support the suspension cables – and the royal dais was way back down the road towards Almondsbury hard by the tolls.

Now, in radio commentaries when there are public speeches you need to talk until the moment when the dignitaries take over from the platform, and this is where the television monitor is a must. Even with binoculars, from my vantage point, it was difficult to see what was going on in the royal box. My television screen gave me a close-up. The then Minister of Transport, Barbara Castle, was to make the introduction to Her Majesty. I reckoned that when the Minister of Transport got to her feet it was a pretty sure sign that she was about to make her introductory remarks and so I shut up and handed over with due deference, but despite the Minister being on her feet it seemed forever before she began her official speech! That pause seemed like an age to the commentator on the day, anxious as he was to cue over at exactly the right moment, but listening to a recording afterwards it was not more than a few seconds. Seconds, though, are the governors of a broadcaster's life.

The difference between the style of the radio commentator and his opposite number of television is so obvious, yet there are some who have yet to learn the technique. The radio man has his eyes, his command of the language and his voice to convey the occasion. Excitement is expressed with the tempo of delivery, like the acceleration or braking of a racing car; he must keep up with the play or the race and convey all the vital information to give a full word-picture of what he sees.

There is a story told of a football commentator – it's probably apocryphal – who missed a vital goal in a league match and rather than admit the error decided to put things right later on. So when play reached the same end where he had missed the goal and play was in an exciting state in front of the goal mouth, he invented the missing goal with all the names of the players who had been involved in the real but missing score! A brave man – if it's true!

That was in the days before television, of course, and it couldn't happen today in sporting events when both radio and television are operating. It is the habit of many people to watch the television pictures but listen to the radio commentary, certainly for cricket. This has something to do with the charm of the commentary team – Brian Johnston and his colleagues who are not merely commentators, but entertainers. They couldn't do the same on television, and this brings me back to my argument. The craft of the television commentator is not knowing when to speak, but when to shut up! His voice is secondary to the pictures; his only job is to guide the viewers through what they can very well see for themselves and there's nothing more annoying for the viewer than to be told something as if it were a gem of wisdom when he or she sitting at home has reached the same conclusion seconds before the commentator puts in his oar.

I may have given the impression that commentating is fraught with danger: no place for the faint-hearted. This is true, up to a point, and I've known some broadcasters voice the opinion that commentaries are not for them. The strain is too great on mind and body. That point of view is understandable and there have been times after a commentary engagement when I have just wanted to creep away and hide. I've even sat in a cinema for two hours – unheard of in my life! Well-meaning people have spoken to me and I haven't heard a word: my mind has been elsewhere, still seeing in my mind the return of Francis Chichester or Alec Rose from round-the-world voyages; the triumphal return of the hulk of the SS *Great Britain* from the Falklands to her original berth in the Port of Bristol or the first flight of the British Concorde. After live broadcasting it takes some time for the flow of adrenalin to subside.

The first flight of the British Concorde prototype 002 on 9 April 1969 was a memorable day. It was not the longest maiden flight – just twenty-two minutes in all from the great Concorde hangar at Filton to the test base at Fairford – but I shall never forget the sight of that enormous silver bird. She flew, with Chief Test Pilot Brian Trubshaw at the controls, with her undercarriage down throughout the flight closely accompanied by her 'chase plane' keeping a watching brief and a photographic record of the historic flight. And as she came into Fairford I was on the edge of the runway in my commentary position looking at an aircraft flying as we had never seen before and landing with her nose in the air in a tail-down configuration. The angle of attack I think they call it, and as I watched I was reminded forcibly of a swan landing on the water, undercarriage down presenting her wings at an angle to provide the maximum braking. That's just how Concorde lands, and I said so at the time, one of those moments when the right words came at the right time.

Many a budding commentator has made the mistake over the years of thinking that the carefully modulated, quiet and reverential delivery was *de rigueur*. The model was that great and talented craftsman in this particular field, Richard Dimbleby. He was the past master of the 'big occasion'. Above all, he was the object lesson to all of us that homework followed by revision and still more revision were the vital adjuncts to successful broadcasts – each of his were finely polished with never a blemish. But such events are precision planned before they take place, as I've indicated. There are other times when you find yourself in at the deep end – like the Beaulieu Jazz Festival or when watching animals.

Foxwatch was a series of late-night television programmes from Bristol which studied the urban fox. Perhaps it's because so much household refuse is nowadays left out for collection in black plastic bags or because some of the old houses have plenty of garden space or perhaps because the wild expanse of the Downs covers a large area of Bristol, but the urban fox is common. There is no doubt in my mind that of all the factors the readily available supply of food from those plastic bags is the main reason foxes do so well. The pickings, let's face it, are much easier from a fox's point of view than in the surrounding countryside. That they've adapted to city life is borne out by their being found with litters of cubs in the most un-foxlike earths, spaces beneath old garden sheds being particularly popular.

So it was that two foxes, a dog and a vixen, took up residence beneath a valuable piece of BBC property, an empty house fronting on to Tyndalls Park Road in the grounds of the Broadcasting House complex behind the Whiteladies Road façade. The Natural History Unit had already carried out experiments with 'see-in-the-dark' infra-red television cameras and used them to great effect from a woodland location in a series watching badgers. But now, to get intimate shots of the foxes in their detached suburban dwelling, it was necessary to have a camera inside the house in the gap under the floorboards where the foxes were moving in. There was no way a cameraman could be inside as well: that would have sent the foxes scuttling off in search of another desirable residence, and so the camera was remotely controlled. Electric motors attached to it would allow zoom and panning facilities. In other words, it was possible to swing through a limited arc as well as obtaining close-up shots. What of the cameraman? He had to learn new techniques to control the camera by using a 'joystick' while sitting in a room of an adjacent building.

The foxes could come and go as they pleased through a hole from their underhouse den into the garden. Their front and only door was alongside the steps leading to the front door of the house and so another camera was needed out there in the garden. With early experiments it soon became clear that the faint hum emitted by the electric motors on the camera inside the fox residence made them slightly wary.

Each time the controls for zoom or pan operated the motors the foxes would prick up their ears, and although we had them under observation for several weeks they never became completely oblivious to the faint noise. It just goes to show how important sound is to fox survival. And for our sound we bugged the place with a microphone.

Dr Stephen Harris of Bristol University was carrying out research into the life of the urban fox and he joined us for the broadcasts, soon reporting that the vixen was pregnant. We first went on the air on 8 May in a programme that was to become compulsive viewing for a large audience over the next eight weeks until the last transmission on 3 July, all of them late at night. On one friday night we didn't go on the air until 1.20am.

In all, eleven programmes were broadcast of the private and intimate life of the fox family, seeing how the cubs grew and developed and became almost adult in a very short space of time. Stephen Harris and I would watch our monitor and listen to the sounds coming from the earth and try to interpret what the various actions meant and the contact calls between dog, vixen and cubs.

When we first looked in on them, the cubs relied entirely on the vixen's milk for sustenance, but very soon we could see by her actions that their teeth were becoming too sharp for her nipples. Shortly after, they were taking solid scraps brought in by the dog fox from his forays into the outside world of Bristol. Then we began to see how the cubs at play were developing into real hunters. The pounce made by one cub onto its brother or sister was but a prelude to the selfsame pounce that would mean a meal in the wild in a few weeks' time. It soon became clear that one cub was emerging as the dominant member of the litter. It was a fascinating study of the city fox family, and for the commentator there was the excitment of never knowing what would happen next in that cosy underworld.

As with any broadcast, there is a story that is never told on the air. The most hair-raising of those late-night broadcasts came in the third week of our *Foxwatch* sequence when I was away from Bristol. I had some time before arranged to spend a week in Scotland with very dear friends who were so helpful in seeing me through the rather dark depths of March when my second wife, Angela, died after a long illness. I wanted to get away from it all and Mike Beynon, the producer of *Foxwatch*, was very concerned and helpful. The holiday haunt was on Tayside, and arrangements were put in hand for me to use the BBC studio at Dundee, for this one wednesday night in May, while Stephen Harris occupied our usual small back room in Bristol.

Rather than drive to Dundee, not knowing the area or precisely the location of the BBC studio, it seemed prudent to order a taxi for ten o'clock that wednesday evening. Ten o'clock came and I was doing my usual pre-commentary walkabout. It always happens – a way of clearing or concentrating the mind maybe, or perhaps just plain worryguts! Shortly after ten o'clock, on going to the hotel reception area to confirm that the taxi would arrive, there was the sight of the tail-lights of the cab disappearing down the drive! The receptionist said something like 'I've sent him away and told him to come back at the right time tomorrow morning! You couldn't possibly want to go to Dundee at ten o'clock at night.' The taxi driver wasn't on radio control, of course, but fortunately he went back to his office some three miles away and by the time he came back a vital half-hour had passed. As soon as the situation had been explained, my Scottish taxi driver warmed to the task and revealed that he had just applied to join the BBC Engineering Department. What a small world! He got me to that small Dundee studio with time to spare and, glory be, waiting there was a splendid bottle of Scotch. As the man who was doing overtime in opening up the studio at unusual hours explained, 'Your producer in Bristol told me that Mr Jones never went on the air without having a drink first.' A slight travesty of the truth, but only very slight.

41

Being in such a remote location there was no chance of my seeing in Dundee the pictures of the *Foxwatch* house *before* we went on the air. My first glimpse would come when the television set in the studio carried the same pictures as those being seen by viewers everywhere. But not to worry, so long as the transmitter didn't break down I could talk to Stephen and he to me, and carry on what was fast becoming a double-act as we watched the fox family. There was the additional back-up of talk-back from Mike Beynon to my earpiece via a telephone line.

Just before we went on the air the law arrived in the shape of a sergeant and a constable on patrol who had seen lights in the studio area at a time of night when the place was usually in darkness and firmly closed. Full marks to them for their observation – but I shall always remember on their entering the premises and casting a look around, their eyes lighted on the bottle of Scotch on the table. Off came their caps and they sat down to make themselves comfortable, delighted to join us in a little BBC hospitality and showing tremendous interest in the broadcast and the technical problems it presented.

The final *Foxwatch* sequence came a few weeks later when the cubs ventured into the outside world. I like to imagine that if they themselves are not alive, then at least their descendants still roam the streets of Bristol.

Paul Nicholas

4
THE WILDLIFE PROGRAMME

It has been my pleasure and part of my further education to introduce every one of the weekly *Wildlife* programmes on Radio 4, which ran for no less than 582 editions, a span of close on twelve years. As with any long-running programme, the poor old front-man gets to the stage where starting the show on a new tack each week taxes the ingenuity and, rather like a stand-up comic in the variety theatre, when the laughs don't come, who starts making fun of the pit orchestra – so I treated my colleagues in the studio. Never, never rehearse the introductions to them – let it come as a surprise! That's the way to get a reaction even if it is nothing more than a groan of woe.

There is another reason for this approach. Sometimes there would be a newcomer, someone with little experience of the world of a radio studio, who would be worried by the isolation of sound-proofing, apprehensive of faces watching through the glass, the cables and microphones, the various cue lights. So my job would be to put them at their ease, make them think that this was nothing more than a cosy chat between friends, which describes *Wildlife* exactly. Put the questions, draw out the answers from the contributors, make them feel at ease, make them enjoy themselves. Thus, hearing their forbidding question-master being slightly flippant in introducing them usually helped in setting the right atmosphere. A few, of course, would always be anxious no matter what ploy one used and there were others who seemed to imagine that my only role was putting difficult supplementary questions. Often such questions would come out but only when I considered that there were gaps or flaws in the answer I had heard. There was never any thought in my mind of bowling one out of the back of the hand to induce a false stroke – more like something of a teasing length!

The naturalists invited to the studio to answer listeners' questions had among their number those who were not averse to springing surprises on their chairman – perhaps it was a form of retaliation for some of the awkward questions. I soon got to know the signs. If anyone appeared with luggage patently beyond the capacity of the usual scientific briefcase and especially a container liberally ventilated with holes, I knew that there was something in the offing.

The questions always went out to our guest speakers well before the broadcast to give them an opportunity to mull them over and in many cases do a little research, but with the proviso that answers heavily written would be out of place: *Wildlife* was an off-the-cuff chat that regarded heavily scripted answers like poison. There were a few who'd produce notes as *aides-mémoire*, but if they persisted in reading those *words* they'd realise in listening to the broadcast that although they might be scientists, they were certainly not members of Equity! Reading a script is a specialised ability given only to those who've spent a lifetime in the business and are able to read while still making it sound extempore.

Having set those guidelines, it wasn't surprising that the better communicators brought to the studio not guideline notes, but animated aids – and I do mean animated! A favourite topic among listeners concerned hedgehogs. Questions were always coming in about their hibernation, whether small ones found late in the autumn would survive and, inevitably, their mating habits! One day during a chat about their spines, one speaker casually bent down and produced from under the studio table a large box. Taking off the lid with the showmanship of a magician, he produced one large boar hedgehog, and carefully placed it on the studio table! This brought the discussion to life as we all enthused, touched the spines (needle sharp if you've never had the chance of checking) and reassured ourselves that any fleas on the animal would not invade the territory of *our* bodies. (Hedgehog fleas live on hogs and not humans.)

We even had a chameleon in front of us one day being fed on laboratory-bred locusts, and there was the evidence of the feeding habits of the animal stalking its prey and flicking out the coiled-up tongue and grabbing the morsel! It persisted in climbing up the microphone with slow, deliberate, sinuous movements and desperately tried to change colour to blend in with the background although in the brightness of the studio, with hardly any shadows, it was hard put to it to find a camouflage in keeping with an alloy mic and black cable!

It may be argued that bringing exhibits to a radio studio was a waste of time and would be more appropriate on television, but that is to beg the question of what radio is all about. It is, above all, evocative. Sounds tell a story and it's a poor broadcaster indeed who cannot find the words to describe a chameleon sitting not three inches from his nose; the enthusiasm in the voice conveys as much as the picture on the screen. Many people prefer a radio play to its visual counterpart. So any exhibits were welcome in the *Wildlife* studio: mounted insects from some long-forgotten museum collection were commonplace as were the skins of British and exotic birds and egg collections usually from the vast resources of the British Trust for Ornithology (BTO); stuffed birds and animals were produced with Houdini-like dexterity from the depths of luggage but it was always the live specimens that produced the 'oohs and ahs'. That studio table had been wandered upon and explored by slow-worm and common lizard, with speakers ever concerned, of course, not to pick them up by the tails! (This is a defence mechanism – they shed their tails if so caught.)

Ladybirds were on the list for one programme, and it so happened that I had discovered a specimen behind the curtains of my house on the morning of the programme. It was mid-winter; so wintery, in fact, that one speaker could not get to Bristol and at the last minute had to be accommodated in the studio at Brighton and linked by line with those which made the Whiteladies Road complex. The ladybird was safely contained in a matchbox and when the question came up I casually remarked on my find and opened the matchbox. 'How many spots does it have?' asked David Streeter in that distant south-coast studio. Sad to say we never found out for the heat of the studio had moved the ladybird from lethargy to mobility and on opening the matchbox it took off and flew to a far corner never to be seen by us again. No doubt it survived and flew out in spring to control the aphids on the BBC roses!

We've also had bats to watch and handle in the *Wildlife* studio. I really can't understand why so many people shudder at the very sight of them for they are such fascinating creatures with wing membranes that look as fine as silk and appear so fragile. Yet they are very powerful fliers. Their bad press stems from the image of the vampire, suggesting blood-sucking from the human throat and the tell-tale twin tooth marks.

One scar I wouldn't particularly like to have is the puncture marks of an adder bite, although I must say there have been experts in the programme who have been bitten and lived to tell the tale. The adder is another animal in the 'least-loved' department, and I must admit that when living in the Blackdown Hills of Somerset some years ago where adders were quite common, I had more than a healthy respect for them. Since then they have moved up my particular popularity chart. At least they had until the day I read a listener's question to the team. I then noticed one of them fumbling in his jacket pocket to produce a small chamois-leather bag. It was carefully tied and had a drawstring. This was released and the bag up-ended and from it slid onto the table a couple of snakes. Slow-worms? Not a bit of it. These were young adders about five inches long, beautiful animals and once again the discussion brightened up as we became more and more enthusiastic about our studio guests trying to make sure they didn't slide towards the edge of the table. The enthusiasm took a sudden downturn, though, when one of those famous Jones supplementary questions was flung in with all the innocence in the world. 'Are those young adders on the table as venomous as those fully grown?' 'Oh yes,' came the answer, 'every bit of it'. There was a slight pause and the rest of the team were very much with me as I gently suggested it might be an idea to return the two snakes to their leather bag. I still like them though.

Many studio exhibits came in the post with the questions: almost anything from tiny beetles discovered in dried pulses to giant wood wasps; exotic beans washed up on some Westcountry shore to mysterious stores of seeds found in the chimney pot. Unfortunately, some listeners would send – with all good intentions I'm sure – carcasses. Now, the carcass of a mouse doesn't travel well through the post during hot weather, and sometimes small parcels would be delivered to the *Wildlife* office at arm's length. There was never a rush to open the day's *Wildlife* packages, particularly after one delivery was found to contain some exceptionally foul excreta!

The studio didn't always confine the *Wildlife* team. Invitations came from many organisations, especially County Naturalists Trusts, to take questions from the members of the audience in the locality. Some of our experts didn't view this with any great enthusiasm since they couldn't have the several days' notice of the questions they enjoyed when in the studio. They had rather nearer thirty minutes, in fact, as the questions handed in at the entrance were sifted backstage and selected into a balanced programme. (We did invite members to send in questions beforehand but this seldom produced more than a handful.)

The size of the audience varied greatly. At the programme at Bristol University to launch the then latest County Trust, the Avon Wildlife Trust, we were faced with some four hundred people in an enormous hall. A trip to Rotherham, however, was slightly different. On arrival, the producer scanned the hall and decided that not enough chairs had been placed for the audience, expected to be in the region of two hundred. With more chairs hurriedly found, the room looked ready to receive the inquisitve audience, all anxious to put questions to our team. But by the time we started, it became fairly obvious as the questions filtered to us backstage that there must be a lack of interest in wildlife and the countryside in this particular locality.

When I went on stage to introduce the programme my worst fears were confirmed. To say the hall was almost empty is very nearly an understatement! But, nothing daunted, we pressed the sparse audience into the first few rows of seats and recorded *Wildlife* in Rotherham. It's rather surprising, but anyone listening to that broadcast would never have known how few people were in the hall. Being close to us on the stage made a cosy, intimate atmosphere, and with the microphone judiciously placed to pick up any applause or reaction from the floor, it could well have been a full house at the Albert Hall!

Rotherham taught us a lesson. Firstly, never to expect an enormous crowd, although as we subsequently discovered there had been a rival attraction on that night, an RSPB event. The second leveller of the ego came much closer to home: the state of the inner man. Since that evening plans, as they say, have been changed. By the time the recording ended it was somewhere near 10pm and the crew, producers, secretaries, team and chairman were in need of sustenance. Not only did we not get an enormous audience that night, we failed to get a good meal. The change of plan dictated that in the future we should have a snack *before* these evening recording sessions of *Wildlife*, but it was noticeable that the production staff kept the fluid content of the meal well down!

Now Morpeth, standing astride the road to the north, was a very different slice of the cake. The meal had been taken before we arrived at the school hall booked for the recording, and our arrival there at about 7pm filled most of us with not just joy but apprehension closely allied to fear. The queue leading to the school was all of a quarter of a mile long. I could see the disbelief on the faces of the team and producers alike. How many questions shall we get and have to sift through before we record? Surely the hall can't accommodate all of them? Should we call the local constabulary just in case? The queue petered out as we entered the school area: not just petered out but seemed to be winding into the building next door. This was not *our* audience, this was something else. The attraction we discovered was far stronger than the magnet of *Wildlife*. It was an exhibition match on the green baize of a billiard table by Alex 'Hurricane' Higgins. You might say we were snookered.

One table we used for *Wildlife* was not of slate but wood. If we're talking about wildlife and countryside topics, why not get out into the countryside went the thinking. Not more than a mile or so from the Bristol studios is the National Nature Reserve of Leigh Woods, liberally littered with marked walks and picnic sites. Our chosen spot was an open space deep in the woodlands where it was still just possible to hear the hum of the city traffic, the occasional aircraft taking off from the city airport, but above all the sound that made the greatest impact was of the birdlife in the trees and the insects buzzing around our heads.

This exercise was repeated but this time we had film cameras hovering around us as persistently as the bumble bees. The Columbia Broadcasting System of America was making a film about BBC radio and homed in on our little excursion in the woods like bees round the hive. Bless the crew, they didn't interfere at all: didn't ask for retakes, didn't complain the camera had run out of film or that the sound man's recording machine had a fault. All common complaints in film circles. We recorded the programme as if they weren't there, which is exactly as it should be.

On this occasion we were recording two programmes, as we would in the studio. One before lunch, one after. Or if things had gone well in the first session, both before lunch with a break for a quick drink between the two. I'm a great one for planning the pleasures of life and I had anticipated that the chances of finding a gin and tonic in the middle of a nature reserve were somewhat slim.

Plans were quickly put into operation. To that idyllic woodland setting went my small hold-all, the one that frequently accompanies me on fishing trips. In it was a supply of the ingredients needed to mix our usual between-programmes refreshment, and the eyes of the team, recording engineers and producer were a delight as this mysterious bag was unzipped. The film crew from CBS was also impressed. Those of us from the British Broadcasting Corporation had come to the conclusion that the American crew had finished filming but to this day I'm not so sure. I've a feeling that the sight of members of a BBC radio programme sitting in springtime in the middle of some woods drinking gin and tonic from plastic mugs was too much to resist!

That piece of film, but without the gin and tonic shots, came back full circle. A BBC series with the title *Do They Mean Us?* picked it up after it had been shown on the CBS Network in the United States. It was screened in a collection of snippets from television organisations all over the world concentrating on British eccentrics. Ah well, if eccentric I be, so be it.

I'm a generous chap, generous to a fault some say, although certain of my good fortunes have to be rationed among only the best of friends. On the nearest recording date of *Wildlife* to the festive season I usually tried to take a little good cheer along to wish my colleagues health and happiness. Derek's sloe gin has become quite famous and, loath as I am to spread its favours too liberally, I'm not so selfish as to keep the recipe to myself.

Pick sloes, sprig them, wash and dry. Here's the tedious bit! Each sloe must be pricked all over with the point of a darning needle. (This operation is sometimes described as 'first kill your sloes'.) Place a tumbler full of these pricked sloes into an empty bottle together with three-quarters of a tumbler of caster or granulated sugar. Fill the bottle to the neck with gin. Keep it in a convenient spot in the kitchen and each time you're near the bottle shake it vigorously. Keep shaking over the days until all the sugar has dissolved and then put it away in a cupboard and forget it until Christmas – if you can!

Some may find my recipe too sweet or not sweet enough so my advice would be to taste the first effort and then vary the sugar ingredient one way or the other. Mind you, these tasting sessions can be disastrous. Before you know where you are the first bottle is empty. Back to the drawing board or back to the blackthorn bushes where you found the last lot of sloes. One day when Chris Mead of the BTO and I were out looking at winter birds the producer left us to record some of the redwings and fieldfares that were clearing a hawthorn hedge of berries. It so happened we were in the middle of scrub liberally littered with blackthorn and plenty of sloes. The plastic bags in which unused tapes reach us were hurriedly pressed into service for gathering sloes. John Harrison had great trouble getting us back to the business in hand of recording a radio programme. But of all the sloes ever collected those picked on Guernsey in the Channel Islands are undoubtedly the lushest, biggest and juiciest I've ever come across. Take a walk in autumn down the water lane leading to Petit Bot: the Guernseymen may have missed a few, but I doubt it!

5
LEPRECHAUNS IN IRELAND

If you should ever go across the sea to Ireland, don't go with any pre-conceived notions that leprechauns are merely the figments of the Irish imagination because it might just happen that some of your best laid schemes go wrong and bother the ordered mind. Blame the little sprites and take it in the faith that Ireland is what Ireland is – unpredictable.

Standard Irish Time, for instance, is akin to a movable feast. Keeping appointments would beggar even the best-organised secretary with the most modern of office computers. My introduction to this particular eccentricity was as one of a team of keen golfers who set out on a safari of those delightful courses and links of Ireland. We were due to meet our first opponents on the first tee at nine o'clock one summer morn: it was Killarney, pure paradise in golfing terms. There we were, getting our golfing swings into shape around the club house as the minutes mounted up to half an hour and the half-hour doubled to the hour, when the first of our hosts appeared, smiling in welcome. 'So you're here already' was his greeting followed by 'Will you be having a drink before we start?' Give up! You'll never beat that attitude to life where time doesn't matter. Join 'em and enjoy it, for enjoy it you will, but for some twenty people from the broadcasting world, where lives are governed by time not in minutes but seconds, it came as a difficult lesson to learn.

There was one autumn morning when producer John Harrison and myself set out at some ungodly hour to meet up with Roger Lovegrove, the RSPB officer for Wales. Our rendezvous was Fishguard and our plan was to board the ferry to Rosslare and on the trip across St George's Channel to take a look at the seabird movement for this was the time of year when one would expect to see many different species moving south to winter quarters. Winter indeed seemed to have arrived from the gales we experienced on the drive through South Wales and the fall of branches along the roadsides. It was not good weather for anyone whose sea-legs go wobbly at the sight of a ruffled millpond.

Rendezvous was made with Roger, and we decided to be circumspect and fill our stomachs on the theory that sailing on a full stomach is 'a good thing'. Two of the party of three also swallowed one of those tiny tablets that help allay the problems of *mal de Irish mer*. Personally, I think it's all in the mind. Any tablet will do the trick if you *think* it's a sea-sickness antidote. However, be that as it may. Three travellers, loaded with luggage and two so-called portable tape machines, boarded the ferry – a splendidly robust vessel, the sort of ship to give one confidence in her sea-worthiness, although at the back of the mind came the reminder, based on journeys to the Channel Islands, that many ferries wallow about like corks.

Confidence waned just a shade on meeting the captain. By way of conversation – and to ease the worried mind – we enquired what sort of weather we might expect on the crossing. (That gale damage on the roads hadn't augured well.) His reply is etched in my mind as permanently as the epitaph on some ancient gravestone. 'I think we shall have a residual swell.' That was the understatement of all understatements ever made.

The crew couldn't have been more helpful; a cabin was put at our disposal, and they made everything easy for we crazy bird-watchers who wanted the best vantage point to pick out our prey. This turned out to be the starboard wing of the bridge, an eerie of a hide with a splendid view for'ard over the bows way below us and the whole sweep of the sea to the north.

Leaving harbour was very pleasant, although we had all taken the precaution of donning full waterproof clothing, the gear always in the boot of my car on *any* excursion into the field (or sea) on natural history recordings be it summer or winter. Just as well we had them this time. Recording started inside Fishguard Harbour as we scanned the inevitable gull population and the ship nosed her way with increasing speed towards the gap in the breakwater. As we left that haven she began to dip her nose. A for'ard glance told us why. That residual swell was swelling.

It was shortly after this that I happened to look at our producer operating one of the tape machines. There were trickles of sweat pouring down his face and his normally healthy colour had changed. Not to put too fine a point on it, he was very pale. He is not a chap to give up in the face of adversity, but at this moment he was facing adversity eye to eye as he muttered something that I didn't catch, but which indicated he was about to disappear below. Now there was a problem. We were committed to record a programme; we had no producer; we should now have to operate the tape machine *and* talk coherently and informatively about the birds braving the gales. For gale it now was!

Sheer fear kept Roger and me going as the ship ploughed on through waves that broke over the bows with such ferocity that we were frequently covered in water even at the height of the wing of the bridge. Fear too of the prophet of that 'residual swell' who was under the impression that two bird-watchers stuck out in the rain and wind should be sustained by Scotch. Roger and I refused dram after dram intent only on keeping ourselves not only sober but as coherent as the gale would allow. It was at this stage that a voice from inside the comfort of the bridge informed us from a slit in the door that the 'swell' had become force ten! We didn't need telling.

Tapes on the machine needed to be changed every twelve minutes or so and that was no easy task squatting down against the cold steelwork of the bridge and hoping against hope that any water falling around us hadn't found its way into the machine. Damp tape machines tend to become duff tape machines. The ploughing match continued into the face of the gale and as far as bird-watching was concerned we had a good bag: something like nineteen different species ranging from gannets to guillemots and even including a vagrant wood pigeon which I'm sure having been given less inclement weather would have perched on a mast or radar stack and hitched a lift across to Ireland.

Rosslare came into view through the driving rain; the swell subsided; Roger Lovegrove and I wound up the recording with a few words that spelt more of a relief than the chosen phrases that should usually end a radio nature trail. At that moment another figure joined us in our eerie. John Harrison, producer, looked at us with an expression that asked a thousand questions, but his concern was patently not for our welfare but whether we had recorded a programme! We had recorded four tapes which should have been enough for his purposes. Now in the safety of harbour, Roger and I proposed to avail ourselves of the hospitality which in the interests of his programme we had shunned for the past two hours. John's remark was a classic. 'That's the first programme I've ever produced and haven't heard more than a few words of it.' He was in fact rather pleased with the end result when he returned to Bristol and listened and edited with his razor blade to put the whole gale-blown near disaster into a shapely programme.

The story doesn't end there. Although we had booked our accommodation beforehand, on arrival we found that the blasted leprechaun was doing his most devilish for the hotel not only had no idea of our impending arrival but they could not offer any accommodation – they were full! Eventually, it was sorted out and we were whisked to another hotel where Roger planned to have a meal with us, before returning on the same ferry to Fishguard. It was a rather rushed affair but a taxi duly took Roger back to the harbour. Knowing that our cabin was still available, he dashed up the gangplank right on sailing time and went straight below to put his head down! Some while later he awoke to feel a stationary ship beneath him and, thinking he had arrived back at Fishguard, went abovedeck. It was at this moment that he was accosted by the 'residual swell' captain enquiring where on earth he'd been as they were waiting to sail! They were still in harbour in Ireland and the ferry had waited for my bird-watching colleague.

The trouble is, leprechauns know no boundaries, being indigenous on both sides of the Irish border as John Harrison and I were to discover couple of days later. Accusations are thrown at the BBC for being super-spenders of the licence fee, yet from personal knowledge, and perhaps loss to the pocket, I know that some producers at least are aware of their responsibilities of cost-consciousness. So it was that the Harrison/Jones combine, lugging the two tape recorders and our wet-weather luggage, besides the necessary clothes to look at least tidy representatives of the BBC at any hotel in which we might stay, headed north from Rosslare for Belfast.

A local taxi driver took us to the station. He was a character, that driver, being like all his fellows not backward in coming forward with the chat. There was BBC plastered all over the tape machine so it didn't need any great intellect to divine our origins. Chatting was his forte, and as there was plenty of time before the train departed he gave us a conducted tour of the port taking in the castle walls as well as a complete history of the place. Being recognised in the streets of Bristol is not unusual, especially the morning after a television appearance, but to be recognised in Rosslare came as something of a surprise. Our taxi driver was a devoted listener to *The Living World* and had put my *voice* to the programme! It was very pleasing, yet rather humbling that someone should be such a discerning listener.

Rosslare Station is more like a 'halt', but the local diesel took us to Dublin where we caught the Belfast train and the journey is to be recommended for any naturalist, particularly bird-watchers, as at many points the line hugs the coasts and takes you through countryside which changes visibly in character between south and north. It's not intended as a criticism, but one *knows* when one is in Ulster by the more concerned approach to agriculture. In the south sodden bales of hay still lay in the fields; in the north, all had been safely gathered in on the day of our travels. But the leprechauns were lying in wait.

Push-buttoning the bedside radio into action next morning for the local news, I heard that a force ten gale was forecast and structural damage might be expected. Not the sort of early morning call you like to hear when you hope to be out in a boat all day on Strangford Lough. Plan B was therefore put into operation. Why not look at the Lough and its natural history from the banks? It was one of those instant Plan Bs that ignored the basic fact that we needed experts to talk on such matters.

Eventually we found ourselves at the local headquarters of people who do research on these Loughside matters and the persuasion of a few pints of Guinness and the promise of a fee produced the men who could talk knowledgeably about sponges and the big fish that come in from the sea. It was wet and it was windy, so much so that I remember closing the programme several times desperately trying to protect the sensitive microphone from the gusts of gale behind a sparse hedge. It worked out in the end but there was a feeling that the leprechauns were blowing like mad all around Strangford Lough.

My most recent encounter with those merry mischievous little sprites was also my introduction to clints and grykes and wedding bells. The characters in this particular story were four tidily dressed chaps all of an age, given a year or so here and there, who met up at Dublin Airport and set out by hire car in a vague westerly direction aiming for one of the most spectacular treasure houses for botanists: the Burren. On the map it looks no great distance as the crow flies, say 130 miles or so, but then Irish crows and Irish roads have a somewhat different navigation system to those of us used to haring hurriedly along motorways. And there is the added brake of a speed limit. So about half-way along our Irish way we were very much in need of refreshment.

The small town of Birr looked inviting, as did an inn in the square. Suitably refreshed we made our thanks, paid the bill and casually enquired of the barman how much longer it would take us to drive to Lisdoonvarna. An innocent enough question since that was our destination, but there was a pause before he made any sort of response. He eyed us up and down, slowly, each in turn. And then said 'So you'll be looking for some wives.'

As some of the party would be bigamists should that be the case, we merely accepted his calculation of distance and left. One of our party was a botanist from Dublin, Charles Nelson, and he could hardly contain his mirth as he explained the barman's remarks. It seems that each autumn Lisdoonvarna gives itself over to the whims of those seeking partners to comfort them through their closing years: computer dating without the need for electronic selection. Just throw them all together and the chemistry that has kept the world population going since Adam picked that apple will sort things out. It's the unmarried small-holders who are the customers, folk without issue who can't bear the thought of not handing on their livelihood to an heir. Further, abhorrence of the idea of the government taking what they have when they die throws them into this oddest of all marriage bureaux. Apparently it works, attracting all sorts of ladies from all sorts of places, including America, and you only have to take in the hotels and guest-houses decorated with wedding bells and horseshoes and other wedding paraphenalia to realise that Lisdoonvarna throws itself wholeheartedly into this annual festival.

We hadn't come to County Clare to investigate the local customs but the local flora in the Burren. This is one of the most fascinating localities I've ever seen in my travels making natural history programmes. Galway Bay is the northern boundary, the sea looking out to the Aran Islands to the west covering an area of 375 square miles: 25 miles east to west and 15 miles north to south. Much of it is limestone pavement criss-crossed by a pattern that makes it seem as if some prehistoric man had been making a stab at laying slabs all over the countryside. Distance is deceiving for the first impression is of a bare landscape devoid of vegetation, but that is far from the truth.

What you have to look into are the grykes between the clints. The clints are the paving stones and the grykes the gaps between them and the dimensions of both vary enormously. Grykes, for instance, may be anything up to a foot across but usually less and as for depth some of them look dark and unfathomable but I'm told that one of 20ft is a deep one. And it's in these crevices or mini-crevasses that the beauty of the Burren shows her natural complexion, adorned only by the make-up of time and wind and weather. You'll find an ash growing there, its roots deep in the gryke, its trunk only as thick as the width of the gryke will allow. Healthy, old and flourishing, but never putting its foliage above the surface where the prevailing wind stunts its growth.

There is the clue that this was once a forest but today each of those gaps between the carboniferous limestone slabs is a woodland in miniature, and some of the slabs themselves are miniature rock gardens for in many of the hollows on their surface colonisation takes place. Lime-loving plants take a precarious hold on the edge of a tiny pool of rainwater. The foliage falls and becomes a frail layer of top soil into which seeds are blown and germinate and they in turn lay down more humus. A rock garden develops and you marvel at the variety of plants.

What in fact we see in both the apparently bare limestone pavements and the well-grassed slopes that form their backdrop is a coming together of plant communities from two vastly different climates, Mediterranean and Alpine. Nowhere else on the Continent of Europe does it occur, this meeting and growing side by side, and the theories behind it are complex. The plant life of the colder north was left behind by ice melting onto an area which before the last glaciation was a warmer climate. Thus the two came together but why they should both survive today is even more complicated. A contributory factor must be the location: the warm air of the Gulf Stream; the ability of the limestone to retain heat; the light – try the light meter on your camera and you'll be staggered to find how bright it is even on a dull day. Thus it is that the Burren attracts the keen botanist, amateur and professional alike, and you can bet that cameras will be found around most shoulders or pressed into the eye at ground level. Seeing such a sight is a sure indication that something unusual has been found whether it is mountain avens, spring gentian or even the Irish orchid. And that particular beauty is one of the prime clues between the Burren and the Mediterranean for I've seen what I *think* is the selfsame on Majorca growing between the rocks beside a road – although not quite the same if you consult the books. The Irish orchid is otherwise described as the dense-flowered orchid (*Neotinea maculata*) whereas the Mediterranean one is *Neotinea intacta*, but just to confuse the issue some books describe *that* as a native of Ireland. But I think it makes my point. In the Burren it's not easy to find but as any flower-spotter knows once you've got your eye in there's no knowing what you'll see.

Like the bird-watching fraternity, there's something of a spy system that operates in the botanical world: rarities are reported through a 'central intelligence agency' and word gets around. It soon became obvious that our hotel in Lisdoonvarna was the 'box' for 'moles'. I hope that Maryangela Keane will forgive my spy analogy; she happens to run the hotel where we stayed and is the acknowledged expert on local flora.

Look at the Burren, love it and respect it. The local feeling is that it is under pressure, although on my visit that was not evident. Perhaps we should not forget the little people and where they may strike next! The signposting for instance is designed to deceive. You'll find them pointing you towards your destination with apparently just five miles to go. The distance could well be five kilometres.

The final idiosyncracy of County Clare during our visit was the telephone system. The only other place I've experienced such service was on the Channel Island of Sark where in the days of the manual 'give the handle a turn' type of communication one didn't ask the lady at the exchange for a number on the island but for the person you wished to speak to by *name*. Being the local clearing-house she knew the whereabouts of all her subscribers. Such quaint local services have disappeared in Sark as they were due to in Ireland, but knowing the country and the people I wouldn't be a bit surprised to find that Maryangela still keeps a bucketful of five pence pieces behind the bar for the customers who wish to make a 'phone call and feed the bulging box with coins. 'How many shall I need for a call to Bristol?' was my enquiry. 'About ½lb.' She was near enough.

We left Lisdoonvarna with some reluctance and some regret — not that a wife hadn't been found for those unencumbered members of the team, but that we had to move on and didn't have the time to take in the Burren more fully. If you have the time and take to the narrow-banked roads, allow plenty of time. You could end up as David Streeter did in our party having to get out of the car and move a herd of cattle before we could get on our way. He'll tell you he walked miles.

6
ORCHIDS IN MAJORCA

I'm a bit of a nut about orchids. This probably dates back to wartime days when a large larch plantation in Somerset was clear-felled to meet the need for pit-props. The year after those trees came crashing down the area of stumps became a carpet of butterfly orchids. It was an amazing sight and goes to show the ability of the orchid seed to survive for what must have been in that case some fifty years and then, when the conditions were right, to germinate and grow into a luxuriant greenish-white carpet.

For sheer orchid exuberance, try the island of Majorca. The first occasion I headed that way was in the course of duty, recording a programme or two for *The Living World*, and since that first visit I've been back at other times to take in not just the flowers of spring but the birdlife too. I'm not suggesting that an instant package to the concrete jungle of Palma will satisfy the hunger of the keen botanist or bird-watcher, but the more northern, less-developed parts certainly will. More to the liking of naturalists is the area around Puerto Pollensa and Alcudia, especially the former, and indeed the tourist industry of the island has cottoned on to the idea of catering for the enthusiasts who want to sample its natural history treasures before the real heat of summer scorches the vegetation. The hotels are full of naturalists during the high season of mid-to-late April. This is when the flora flushes and the migrant birds fly in and top up their fuel tanks on the mass of insect life before heading north for their summer nesting quarters.

One of the charms of Majorca is that you don't have to wander very far from your hotel to find a veritable wild flower garden on any bit of waste or wetland that hasn't as yet been tormented by the developers, for make no mistake some of the island has been irretrievably lost in natural history terms. The old, old story of man pushing outwards from his enclaves and pushing back the frontiers of the wild.

But back to the orchids – even these will be found on slender open spaces with high-rise hotels as their neighbours. Serapias is probably the commonest in such situations (*Serapias parviflora* mainly), reddish and violet in colour. Bee orchids can be found too, and one that has really taken evolution by the scruff of the neck and made sure of its survival by the difficult expedient of getting the best of all worlds. This is the mirror orchid or mirror-of-Venus. Now it's a fact that many orchids imitate insects – bee, bumble-bee, fly – in order to attract those insects and thus pollinate them. The mirror is aptly named since its lip has a centre of bright blue which, the theory goes, acts like a mirror and thus *any* insect landing on it will think it not a reflection but a mate, and in the way of the world the orchid will be pollinated. It's one of the craftiest bits of adaptation, and by the profusion of mirror orchids it's tempting to think they might take over the island!

Those are of small stature, but don't imagine that with all orchids you need to walk warily for fear of treading them to destruction – there are some that are anything but knee-high to a grasshopper, including two in widely differing habitats, woodlands and wetlands. Keen botanists and bird-watchers alike will make for the marshes or salinas (salt pans) and there against a backdrop of reed beds you'll find the impressive loose-flowered orchid, *Orchis laxiflora*. It's enormous, standing up to 3ft tall, and its colour varies from red to pink. It's the queen of the marshland orchids. The king, though, is found in woodlands and once again it's the combination of colour and height that attracts the attention. Yet despite the size, it's very easy to miss them through not having the eyes trained to observe, for seen at a distance they could be dismissed as sapling pines. This is *Limodorum abortivum*, sometimes known as the violet bird's-nest orchid, and the popular name is apt since its flowers are deep violet in colour. Once the eye is in, a patch of pines will yield dozens of them and should you be tempted to come back next day when perhaps the flowers will have opened more and make a better photograph, forget it. Twenty-four hours later the orchid standing like a cane in the woodlands could have wilted. Take those photographs when you find one, then you won't be disappointed in an orchid of the woods, dark and mysterious, which may be a parasite or a saprophyte.

Orchids are almost a fetish for some people. I must confess I fall into this category, for their study will not reveal to me all their mysteries. More, many more than I've mentioned will be found in Majorca. One last word on the subject. There is one that is quite rare, the bug orchid and the experts will tell you that it has a distinctive smell – of bed bugs. Not even the most naive will say 'Oh yes, so it does.' Who is going to admit that they *know* what bed bugs smell like?

Spare a glance, though, for some of the other beauties. Cyclamen may be easily found tucked away under a rocky outcrop, with tiny delicate flowers. More spectacular but less easily found these days is the peony, but if you should take the twisting mountain road from Puerto Pollensa to Formentor these may be found in a runnel that occasionally flows with water just short of the tunnel near the highest point of the drive. A word of warning, though, that the only available parking space will probably be taken up by a coach full of botanists looking for the self-same flower. If you don't find it, just admire the myriad wild rock gardens – they are gems.

If there is one flower that really is eye-catching but makes you wonder if you had a drop too much of the local brandy the night before, it is the cytinus. This is a parasite on the many many acres of cistus (rock rose) that abound on the island. The first clue that it is parasitic in habit is the lack of green leaves. In appearance it's rather like a flamboyant fungus, pushing its way through the soil and growing only to mushroom height with lemon-coloured flowers surrounded by orange-red scales. The day I first saw it with a party of botanists, we were attracted by the familiar praying circle of photographers, bottoms in the air, close-up lenses aiming inwards, the 'rarity signal' that you soon get to recognise on these tours! Indeed, the circle gets so crowded that some have to wander away and find their own specimens and then the clever ploy is to find something that the circle hasn't found. They'll rush over to you in a rodeo-like rush. Show them your find and wander quietly back to where the circle was in prayer and you have the area to yourself without having to worry about the shadows of other photographers interfering with your shot! It was on just such an occasion that someone found a tiny tortoise! That brought them running!

Majorca is rather like a high-speed, self-service cafeteria for the spring migrant birds who drop in and use it as a stopping-off-cum-topping-up point on their long journeys from south of the Sahara to who knows where they may have their chosen nesting sites on our own and other

European shores. Most striking of all are the swifts, swallows and martins, hawking in their millions over the marshes and salinas of the island picking off in flight insects breeding in profusion in such damp places. (You'll find some of the insects have a hunger too – for us! If you're at all susceptible to mosquitoes taking a sip of your blood, go well prepared with repellent or treatment. This is one of the few places where people who normally scorn your smoking habits tend to walk by your side when the cigarette helps keep away some of the insect predators!)

Among the mass of birds there are some strangers to our eyes. Lighter in colour than the familiar swift is the pallid swift and the giant of the group, the alpine swift, with its distinctive white underparts. Similarly, there could be crag martins which are local nesters, doing presumably what house martins did before they found the convenience of our houses on which to plaster their mud – nesting high up on valley and sea cliffs.

The marshes, too, give a sight of such birds as the little egret, brilliant white in the clear Majorcan air, and one day I came across the bird-watcher's equivalent of the botanist's prayer-ring when the object of telescope and tele-photo lens was a bird considered a bit of a rarity thereabouts, a squacco heron.

The birdlife of Majorca is endless: nightingales singing outside your window day and night; the warblers, fan-tailed, Cetti's, Sardinian and Marmora's, which looks so like the Dartford warbler. There are some birds, though, that give themselves away by sheer size rather than distinctive song. Sadly, the black vulture is declining in numbers – indeed it is one of the Continent's endangered species – but it is still possible to see them in spring, high in the sky above the mountain peaks with great straight outstretched wings. Flying barn-doors was the description Chris Mead of the British Trust for Ornithology gave them – that's just about it.

Marsh harriers are found in some numbers fortunately

(among those insect-ridden marshes again), and it's nothing to see half a dozen flipping over the reeds at the same time, then flopping out of sight. And above them with the frequency of a regular bus service from the mountains to the sea will come an osprey. The happiest memory of my most recent visit to Majorca was of such a bird. The coach taking us to the airport waited outside the hotel not much more than spitting distance from the bay. There was the usual panic that seems to accompany such departures – someone missing, someone else had left behind a piece of luggage. Day was fast fading to dusk as we looked out to sea for the last time. Not more than twenty yards offshore there was a large splash and, struggling from the water, was an osprey with a large fish clasped tightly in its talons. It was almost as if to say 'Now there's a memory of Majorca to take away with you.' Unforgettable.

One bird, though, mystifies many a visitor and they talk over breakfast in hotel restaurants of the noises in the night outside their bedroom windows. 'It just seemed to go on and on – a sort of mechanical noise.' It can be a bit monotonous, the call of scops owl, for that is what our unsuspecting fellow guests had been hearing during the dark hours. These tiny birds often sit in the palms, absolutely impossible to see even with a powerful torch, but hear them you most certainly will. So keen were John Harrison, Chris Mead and myself that we set out from the hotel sometime after eleven o'clock one night when the owls were at their most vocal. We were determined to get close to one and obtain a really clear recording. We walked along darkened streets past even darker villas and found ourselves getting closer to one owl. We pressed on and it was obvious that the bird was in the grounds of a large building in front of us surrounded by a high wall and even higher trees. So we 'hushed' and got a splendid recording of scops owl. It was only then, the machine switched off and congratulating ourselves on our enterprise, that we noticed two figures at the gate of the building. Two figures, armed, with rifles! Spanish Police Barracks! We felt it time to leave.

One of the mysteries of the Mediterranean still puzzles people who return there year after year and wander along the sandy beaches with their picnic baskets and bikinis. As they mooch along the tide line, you can see them skirting around lines and heaps of sandy-coloured balls. I've even seen them lightly – even gingerly – kick them with a sandalled toe, visibly determined not to touch them with their hands. It's almost as if they think them the droppings of some herd of animals that has passed that way. They never consider that there are no tracks leading either towards or away from these rather objectionably round, flattened balls. They shouldn't worry. These are the result of tidal actions and they are nothing more than a tightly mangled mixture of sand and fibre known colloquially as 'sea-balls'. The fibrous content comes from neptune grass, an underwater plant, *Posidonia oceanica*, and when the leaves break off and decay wave action produces the apparent droppings on the shore. The people of Majorca have a rather crude sense of humour and the local name for sea-balls suggests an association between nuns and breaking wind!

For birds and botany my sights are firmly on Majorca, but for butterflies my Mecca would have to be the Mediterranean coast of France, although on one trip for *The Living World* I could cheerfully have turned tail and caught the next available flight out of Nice. We had just arrived, the producer and I, and booked into our hotel at Le Luc to find that the hotel had a beautiful garden restaurant set among gentle lighting under the trees, with a bar in an open-ended room. Imagine our surprise when the 'room' moved and was slowly wound back to become nothing more than a canopy over the bar. Ingenious! Now everyone was in the open air. We weary travellers settled down to our meal with, of course, a good bottle of French wine. My meal was of the daunting size – a bowl overflowing with crayfish. About half-way through them, a waiter was seen passing by with a silver salver on the edge of which perched a thrush. But the bird didn't move – it just perched. Then the penny dropped. This was a stuffed bird and it was followed by several more similarly served. Of course, what was happening was that some diners were having a pâté made of thrush tongues and to persuade the customers that they were getting the real thing the stuffed thrush decoration was added. It's a repulsive habit and I was so indignant I couldn't face the rest of my meal. Another aspect of the place worried me. How as it, with a balmy evening among the trees and lights all round, that we weren't bothered by a single insect? There must have been some insect repellents or killers to deter them.

A couple of days later we found ourselves in Sospel at the foot of the Alpes-Maritimes north of Nice, in a sturdy hire car heading for the hills. We had to stop several times, not just to look at the superb views but because the car found it heavy going with three people aboard. (We had met up with Frank Perring by this time.) It was a case of leaving the driver to push on up the track, for it was nothing else than a single-width cart track as we climbed higher and higher, the sort of track that would turn into a raging torrent should the heavens open. It was worth every stone-crunch on chassis to get up there among the Alpine meadows: a magic carpet of flowers, the sort of meadows *we* used to have too before we fertilised and weed-killed and re-layed them into green mono-grass. Being so full of orchids and daisies, trefoils and parsleys, there were insects buzzing and flitting from flowerhead to flowerhead in the happy ecstasy of summer. It's not that many of the species of butterfly were different from those familiar to us: the peacocks, painted ladies, tortoiseshells and fritillaries, but there were just so many more of them. It was nothing to find a dozen of several different species all busy at the flowers of a yarrow plant. Of course, we did come across some strangers to our eyes. One that appears completely black in colour when flying is the dryad. And there was that gloriously gaudy swallowtail

71

which oddly didn't seem as common as its cousin, the scarce swallowtail, which had wing appendages less pronounced than the ordinary swallowtail.

We managed on that rough-riding trip to run out of track and had to foot it through the tree-line out on to the open mountainside, and who would believe, here at something over an altitude of 4,000ft to find a notice indicating cheese for sale. There, out on the plateau, a farmer lived the summer through with his herd and made cheese on the spot. I can't imagine he had many customers! This was being next to heaven. We'd left behind the wooded valleys, the alpine meadows; this was the other world of orchids, slight in stature and, even slighter, the ground-clinging edelweiss. As if we hadn't drunk our fill, there was more to come. From various points on the mountain's slopes came strident alarm calls of marmots, those small mountain rodents, on sentry duty. We sat, we looked, we listened – and we were happy.

That evening we relaxed in the warmth of the evening outside the inn in Sospel and remembered the day and told and retold the story of the journey in the car up the mountain, and as we sat there was another reminder of how much richer are some countries than our own as we watched the masses of moths flying around the street lights and bats in their dozens hawking in taking *their* evening repast.

We did take in one other part of France, Provence. And if you want to be overwhelmed by sheer numbers of butterflies, go there. Try the little town of Apt and find a small hotel overlooking the square and sit on a balcony to have your evening meal. A word of warning, when we were there it seemed to have been taken over by a French Steptoe convention. The square and all the side streets were littered with stalls and every imaginable piece of junk. But there was obviously a market for it. Next day, head for the hills outside the town and feast your eyes and permeate your nostrils in the lavender fields. Now they really are a butterfly paradise.

I've become something of a francophile, not just because I enjoy the food and the wine but because so much more of their countryside than ours has survived in the traditional way. Peasant farming doesn't produce the way of life of the barley barons but it has preserved more of the wildlife in all its forms. Folk will argue that the French are shot-gun happy and pop off at anything that moves. Maybe. But they do produce splendid booklets for the guidance of hunters on do's and don'ts and details of protected species. So, *Le Petit Livre Vert du Chasseur* may be ignored by many, but so long as the Alpes-Maritimes are untouched I'm prepared to forgive – but *not* the stuffed thrush on the side of the silver salver!

7
MAGIC MOMENTS

It has always been my firm belief, confirmed by more years than shall be revealed spent in the countryside, that going out to *find* wildlife is a dead duck. To succeed in that respect you'd have to have the country craft of a poacher who's never been up before the beak, a Red Indian tracker, coupled with a wile and stealth of Charles James, the Fox. And even then, with all those attributes rolled into one superrefined collection of the senses, the prey would be equally alert, equally qualified in country craft. Just think, that's the equation of survival where x is the survivor. But just one of the ploys used by wild predator and prey will stand the human observer in good stead – standing still and saying nothing. Wildlife then comes to you.

There was a classic example of this on a recent trip to the Elan Valley in central Wales with two members of the RSPB Welsh Office, Stephanie Tyler and Roger Lovegrove. They joined us on what appeared at first sight to be the worst possible time of year for bird-watching, early December. The worst possible location too for that matter: the main road through the valley which in summer would be teeming with traffic. Winter, though, changed all that. The vehicles were few, local and far between. Yet standing on that roadside the birds came to us. One side of the road fell away through sallow and plantation edge to a reservoir. The other sloped up to the sky with the occasional weather-blasted oak and birch. Long-tailed tits were our first visitors, a flock of them trapezing on twigs with their slender bodies, searching for life in the buds with the urgency that a December day must generate in a world where the loss of food means death. Then the tiny contact call of the tits became a signal to others: a treecreeper in the oak, no two. There are three of them! And there's a nuthatch in the same oak, no, there are two! Is that a coal tit? And blue tits! Listen. Goldcrests. Where? There, in the birch. All that happened to us while we stood and watched, but even then those tiny birds were so intent on feeding and presumably feeling safe in their numbers that we were able to walk and talk between the verges and not a bit of notice did they take. It's a salutary lesson.

That particular area of Wales now blessed with the title of the County of Powys but which I still regard as Radnorshire, has given me other examples of the unexpected, turning up out of the blue. Roger Lovegrove has shared in all these experiences – like the day we sat on a hillside idly chatting, when two birds of prey came over a high rocky outcrop at some considerable altitude. Binoculars were immediately focussed into the high distance and the first glimpse produced the same deduction of a couple of buzzards indulging in aerial play. The second look showed that the higher of the two birds had a forked tail. Some buzzard! What we were privileged to watch was a buzzard and a red kite playing an 'I'm the King of the Castle' game in the skies. We hadn't searched for them; they had come our way. The same thing happened one day with a peregrine falcon which gave me the finest view imaginable of this majestic bird of prey, immediately overhead in silhouette which confirmed the oft given description of 'an anchor in the sky'.

And then there was one very wet and flooded spring day when we were walking along the banks of a river and looking at last year's nesting holes in the sandy bank of the sand martins, long gone to Africa and soon due back to continue the life cycle that demands that they commute such great distances. As we looked and as we talked of their imminent return, first one, then another and a third sand martin came flitting up stream and in a chatter of excitement each of them made for separate nest holes! It wasn't a case of investigating the site before flying in, they made a bee-line for the holes; they knew exactly where they were heading but how many thousand miles had they made to that particular destination? It was a remarkable demonstration that being 'bird-brained' doesn't mean an inferior intelligence. There's no doubt in my mind that those sand martins knew exactly where they were – home.

If orchids are my passion in wild flowers, when it comes to the freedom of the air birds of prey are the winged aristocrats, a view that runs quite contrary to all that my younger days and paternal edicts taught me. Gamekeepers, and both my father and grandfather were of such respected calling, waged wholesale war on them. In retrospect, that is understandable since the methods of rearing game birds in coops in open fields made a ready harvest for any sparrowhawk, for instance, to nip over the hedge of the rearing field and pick off a pheasant chick at will. So, instead of changing the system, the keepers killed the culprits. Fortunately the system has changed, though not to my mind entirely for the better. Nowadays they rear birds that have been bred in large numbers in the confines of closed pens where each chick is the enemy of its kin and indulges in the habit of plucking the feathers out of the tail of its neighbours. The law today, though, takes care as far as it's able of the plight of the birds of prey.

A sparrowhawk is a thing of beauty with an instinct to kill and survive that seems in conflict with its charms. See one nip over a fence and pick off an unsuspecting small bird with the precision of a laser beam and then away over the next fence, up and over in a thrice. See it, but blink if you dare for that could mean missing the experience. Driving down a narrow country lane recently gave me the supreme demonstration of the sparrowhawk's speed and mobility of flight. It was one of those lanes that flows fast with water during the winter rains, with high banks and hedges on both sides and merely token space along its stretch for cars to pass on an otherwise single track. The hawk dashed down in front of the bonnet and preceded me for almost a mile until the lane joined a road of more major proportions. I tried to keep up with the hawk and found the car doing more than 30mph with the bird outpacing me. All the time it was no more than six inches from the road surface, in fast, meandering flight, the blue-grey feathers of the back and wings giving it away as a cock bird. I can only assume it was stalking for any small bird that might have been dusting in the sand or bathing in the water held by many pot-holes, and one can only assume too that that bird had tried the trick and been successful on many previous flights. Came the end of the lane, where in the interests of safety, I had to halt. Not so the sparrowhawk. It gained just enough height to miss any car and was up and over the far bank hedge in a flash to be seen no more. I still have to pinch myself to remind me that this was no flight of fancy.

Two 20mm shells are trophies on my mantelpiece, among the many other odds and ends that remind me of places I've been and things I've seen. The sort of 20mm ammunition fired in anger from the cannons of fighting aircraft of the Armed Forces. These two are not given pride of place as a glorification of war, rather of the tolerance of wildlife to what man is doing with the world. Out on a remote part of the South Wales coast is an Air Weapons Firing Range where, in carefully briefed and controlled operations, pilots may practice with live ammunition ground attack, firing their weapons at a well-defined yet small target. About 100yd to one side of the target is a tiny control tower where the staff are in radio contact with the pilots and can tell them of the success or otherwise of their aim. The noise is horrendous even inside the thickly glazed tower: the noise of screaming jet engines and the staccato bursts from 20mm cannon rend the air and threaten the ears. It takes some believing, but a kestrel sat on one of the marker posts not 50yd from the target with the sound of an approaching Hawker Hunter clearly audible and nipped off the post to the ground as the aircraft 'whooshed' over at a height of no more than 50ft. There came the crash of the cannon followed by the whine of the jet as the pilot pulled for altitude out to sea. 'Roger Charlie 3 – on target' went the message from the tower. At that moment the kestrel calmly flipped back to its vantage point on the marker post.

The staff at RAF Pembrey are keen on the wildlife around them in what was a nature reserve. Members of the public are firmly kept out – who would be fool enough to put even a foot inside an area where 20mm shells fly about? It's not just the birdlife, but the flora too and there are well-documented records of all the range has to offer thanks to the enthusiasm of the tiny RAF station. It proved to me that wildlife is tremendously tolerant and becomes used to noise and intrusion. The fact that birds of prey were there shows that the pickings of small mammals must be good. The clue is that people are absent, buildings just about non-existent, but the open spaces remain. The staff there do boast that on that marker post I watched, a hen-harrier would take perch and into the target area would fly the other Harrier, the RAF or Royal Navy jump-jet. Harrier on ground, Harrier in the air – perhaps I'll see it one day.

Our respect and admiration for birds of prey is underlined by the aircraft industry today in turning to these winged aristrocrats in the search for names for aircraft, names synonymous with speed and agility in the air. The Harrier is a case in point and so too the jet trainer used by the Red Arrows Aerobatic Team, the Hawk. Let us not forget the Rolls-Royce engines used to power the aircraft down the years and surely the most famous was the Merlin, contributing enormously to victory in the Second World War in such famous aeroplanes as the Hurricane and Spitfire, the Mosquito and the legendry Lancaster bomber. That Merlin took its name from our smallest bird of prey, a bird seldom seen, but I did meet up with one on an autumn day on the edge of Exmoor. It was one of those days when the binoculars were not in the car and a heap of National Park Committee notes would hardly bring a strange bird into focus. Fifi (for she is a French car) needed refuelling and my chosen garage was one regularly used on that journey. As petrol flowed into the tank, I happened to glance across the road and found my eyes zooming in on a small tree not more than 30yd away. On its top was a bird, perched just as a little owl would perch on a telegraph pole. That, indeed, is what I thought it was as the sun caught the flecked or streaked plumage, but then a few more cogs in the gear of my mind meshed into place and reminded me that little owls have nothing more than an apology for a tail. At that moment a kestrel came up to the tree and 'buzzed' its occupant with no little aggression, and my striated feathered-friend disappeared. What I had been watching on that tree was a young merlin. Every time a call is made at that garage I glance across the road in the hope that it might be there again. So far disappointment, but one day . . . And next time my binoculars *will* be in the car. It taught me a lesson.

One of the great joys of the countryside is that you don't necessarily have to have a sighting of a bird or a mammal to experience some of the thrills of the wild. Some sounds can tingle the spine: the distant bark of a fox on a moonlit night in January; the single yap of a roe deer in spring; the belling of a red deer stag of an early autumn morning on the edge of a moorland combe. Calls that all have a meaning, some with mating, others with warning or the proclaiming of territorial rights. Other sounds are pure magic, like the mewing of a buzzard high over the hills circling and spiralling the thermals or the croak of a raven – two calls that draw the eyes to the heavens to scan the sky for the graceful birds stating their rights or contacting a mate.

For sheer cacophony of sound there's nothing to match a colony of birds on a small rocky island: it's like being in the middle of an orchestral rehearsal without a conductor and each musician not only out of tune but determined to play a different melody from his neighbour. But when birds are in such close proximity they have continually to defend each tiny individual nesting site from the next that is only a beak peck away. There are birds that get over the problem of physical contact by nesting underground. Even then, noise plays a part in their lives. It's much like putting a 'sold' notice over the estate agent's board. Sorry, this property is no longer available. I'm thinking of that graceful bird of the oceans, the Manx shearwater, and there's one island where they gather for nesting each year in enormous numbers, Skomer off the coast of Pembrokeshire. Just look at the housing problem. On an island of around seven hundred acres, a population of Manx shearwaters of, say, a hundred thousand pairs. That's an awful lot of birds for a small housing estate. On a dark night in late spring they certainly make their presence felt, or rather heard. It's weird to hear diabolical chuckles coming from a hole in the ground and screams from the birds buzzing around your head. That in itself is frightening, but their senses must be sure for I've never had a bird-strike from a single one. Come the morning you'd think the birds had flown, for all is as silent as the grave. No chuckles, no screams.

There is no chance of seeing them during the day when most visitors land on Skomer but you will certainly see the burrows, once the warren of rabbits, and it's fairly easy to put an unwary foot into such a hole and sprain an ankle. Easier still at night in the darkness, but then not many visitors spend the night on Skomer unless they are scientists researching or broadcasters broadcasting. Anyway, the accommodation is limited on this National Nature Reserve to the Warden's house and part of the old, ruined farmhouse, but to spend a night there is an experience never forgotten.

It's not just the sheer weight of numbers of the shearwaters but their lifestyle that makes you wonder about the lengths to which some species have to go to be successful in the evolutionary system. Here's a bird that is nocturnal and nests in an old rabbit burrow. Incubation of the eggs takes about 51 days and the parent birds share the duties. One stretch of egg-duty will last for 6 days before the mate returns from sea to take over. Even after those 51 days there's the chick to feed and that is another long-term sentence; 10 weeks of solitary for the chick, on anything but bread and water, rather a fish-fattening diet to build them up for their maiden flight and that is about 6,000 miles in distance to off-coast South America.

Incidentally, Skomer is looked after by the West Wales Naturalists Trust, and if you should visit the island observe their advice and respect their concern for this splendid nature reserve. Keep to the trails and don't venture into a nesting gull colony – you're quite liable to have a scar on the head if you're not wearing a hat. Gulls have a nasty habit of 'buzzing' any intruder and blood may be drawn – yours, not theirs.

Skomer is rather a special case. There you know you can see the gulls nesting on their inland sites surrounded incongruously by a carpet of bluebells, the kittiwakes on tiny cliff ledges, narrow and precarious; puffins, too, though their numbers have declined and inland near the wetter parts you may be lucky and spot the low hawking flight of a short-eared owl. All that is predictable and a pleasure never to be forgotten. I still go back to my unexpected encounters as the ones that really give the bonus – the free issue for the wildlife investor.

Never have I seen a bittern in the wild, that 'boomer' of a heron so rare in our countryside and found, or perhaps heard, in areas of reed beds. All the books describe its habit of pretending to be a reed when disturbed by thrusting its beak, head and neck straight upwards and thus, with its colour, looking rather like the reed stalks in the background. The pictures are most convincing, but those given the chance of seeing it in the wild must be blessed with abnormally good eyesight as well as good luck. One day there came news that a bittern, a young one, had been injured on a road and was now at a sanctuary run by the RSPCA. Outside Taunton in a shed at the sanctuary was the bittern, and the warden had placed in the corner a goodly bunch of reeds. Looking inside, imagine my surprise to find one young bittern, body pushed against the reeds in the corner with bill, head and neck pointing to the roof! A classic camouflage and something I dare say I shall never come across in the wild. The bird, even in that shed, blended so well into the background that I realised trying to spot it with binoculars around the edge of a reed bed would demand more than one's life-share of luck.

Good eyesight I am blessed with except when it comes to reading the morning papers when, without extending arms or using spectacles, I'm hard put to it to read much more than banner headlines. Thankfully, anything beyond arms-length distance is sharp and clear. That has stood me in good stead over the years from spotting lost golf balls nestling in the rough to a day I was walking over Dorset heathland and came upon the shed horn of a roe deer. These, like the antlers of the larger deer such as fallow or red, are seldom found although they are discarded every year to make way for bigger more imposing growth (until the declining years set in). The reason is re-cycling. From their own horns or antlers deer obtain calcium. In the case of the two-pointer picked up in Dorset nibbling had already started, so much so that one point was needle sharp. Small mammals, too, will take advantage of this vital chemical supply.

Maintaining territory in the wild is one of the factors in the survival equation, and many and varied are the ways of proclaiming that a particular niche is occupied, be it by vigilant patrolling, marking boundaries with urine or more visible signs, or by audible sounds. It's surprising how deeply the territorial instincts extend in the animal world. Many insects for instance, like some of the butterflies and dragonflies, are intent on keeping out their neighbours of the same kind. Stand in a spot where you've seen one of the big hawker dragonflies in perhaps a woodland ride and this helicopter of the insect world will fly to and fro in an iridescent frenzy. *You* are in its air space.

I hadn't really thought about it until I was taken to part of the New Forest to look for some of our native reptiles, but they are also territorial. It was Ian Spellerberg who led this snake safari with the intention of finding that rarest of our reptiles, the smooth snake, and adders, our only venomous snakes. Mind you, Ian had made an extensive study of the area in the course of his work at Southampton University but I was more than surprised when walking through the Forest he said, in effect, 'Quiet now, turn left and twenty yards down the path there's a conifer and under it we should find an adder.' Such instructions needed no repeating. Round the corner, woodsman-type walking, not a sound, so quiet it was possible to hear the very faint sound of the motor in the tape recorder. Sure enough, under a solitary pine was the adder curled up in a tight coil with head in the centre and eyeing us. We started talking about the discovery and the snake quietly slid away into the undergrowth. 'Oh yes,' said Ian. 'That one's usually here on a morning like this – they're very territorial.' Likewise we found a smooth snake, but that was a bit more difficult for they are very scarce. The encounter with the adder, though, is something that should be borne in mind by anyone venturing into the countryside and having a morbid fear of being bitten. Adders are more concerned to get out of our way than we are of being bitten by them. If there are adders along your walk you can be pretty certain they'll be long gone before you reach the spot where they were taking the sun. The only danger time is in the spring and autumn when the snake is somewhat lethargic on coming out of hibernation or getting ready for the long winter sleep.

The proclamation of territory by birds is obvious. It happens not just in the great fanfare of the dawn chorus in spring but at other times too. There is nothing more vibrant of the promise of spring than a song thrush singing lustily atop a tree on a sunny morning in December on days before even the first fall of snow; or a robin gently whispering its sub-song on the same December day. It's a moment to remind yourself as you snuggle back into the duvet that you come a very poor second in the survival stakes. Perhaps we should hibernate and forget the problems of heating and lighting bills!

8
BEING AN EXPERT

You're expected to be an expert when you're regularly heard introducing natural history programmes. Although I can't claim to be any sort of expert, I do take pride in trying to help anyone with a problem of identification or explanation of anything unusual, to them, in the countryside. And I do this being convinced that if anyone shows the *slightest* interest in wildlife then the future is that much brighter. Someone once said that knowledge is not having information at your fingertips but knowing where to find the answer, and so all my many reference books are well used and well thumbed and some have been carried from home to the pub round the corner for that is where many of the queries arise. What I really need is a second copy of all my books behind the bar!

There was one dear old man, long since departed to his wild gardens, who lived a lonely life deep in the countryside. Here was a chap who knew more than he was prepared to admit, a happy man who every day made a long trek on foot down a narrow lane to collect groceries from the shop and stock up his frail body with the liquid sustenance it seemed to need. He always described that lane, full as it was of wild flowers in the spring, as 'his garden' and in retrospect I'm sure that his dog and the stray, near-wild cats and the local bird population at his home fed better than he did. He was that sort of man, a man with a concern for the countryside. He always heard the first cuckoo in April; the first swallows looked into the old outbuildings round his home before they investigated any other site; spotted flycatchers were almost his personal property. He didn't have to see an SFC, as he called them; he *heard* them in the lane, the sound of the snapping of their bills as they took an insect on the wing. He was right about that – it's a very distinctive sound. By his keen eye the first nest in the area of the SFC would be his little secret as well as the leafy nests of jenny wrens. He used his eyes and his ears, and although he would never show you the nest sites it was always a challenge to trace his daily walk and try to track down his treasures. He'd turn up with flowers asking what they could be, always knowing full well the answers. The classic he tried on me was a tiny, near-white flower and I had the instant feeling that here was something not quite right. This wasn't a complete flowerhead, this was a floret from something larger and more luxuriant. 'Cow parsley' I said after due consideration of the facts in front of me and the character of the man. A great laugh welled from deep inside and the eyes smiled almost to tears as he said. 'You'm right Derek.' A great character and a good countryman.

It's always enjoyable to be able to tell a gamekeeper something he doesn't know, particularly as most of them are pretty good naturalists. On this occasion luck had smiled. One of my regular walks takes me between some woodlands, keeping an eye on a heronry, and through a field in which there's an old pond – one of those that has no visible supply of spring or stream water yet is full to overflowing during winter months thanks to drainage from the surrounding fields and in summer is near bone dry. One late autumn day about 20yd from the water, three birds towered into steep flight uttering a triple alarm call – sharp and piercing – and there was a bright, white flash from their rumps as they took off. A few days later the keeper asked about a bird he had seen which looked like a large house martin. When asked where he'd seen this he indicated it was the selfsame pond. I'd looked up my sighting in the books and suggested he'd seen a wood sandpiper. It adds to your stature when you can come up with the instant identification!

Diplomacy, though, must often be exercised in handling some situations, and although you may never have the proof of good intentions making the effort is the important factor. A local and very old farm came up for sale and inevitably went to a developer whose first action on the property was the demolition of some of the barns and sheds. They were all falling into disrepair, but had been good wildlife habitat. My concern was for the village bats of which there are some considerable numbers but there was no proof that they used these old buildings. Enquiries about finding any of these small mammals during the course of the builder's work produced nothing more than a blank 'Bats? What do they look like?' I'm not that naive to think that a speculative builder hasn't heard of or seen bats during his lifetime so the PR approach was called for. The next day I gave him a copy of the Nature Conservancy Council's booket *Focus on Bats, their Conservation and the Law.* To my surprise, the builder became quite enthusiastic about the photographs and, having got his interest, I pointed out the legal requirements of bat conservation. I shall never know whether any bats were disturbed in the course of his work, but at least an effort had been made.

'I've found a bat in the churchyard porch, it's dead and it has a numbered tag on one wing.' So went a 'phone call one early May morning from a man who keeps more than a fatherly eye on a church in the Gordano Valley. Mr Knight on the 'phone, reckoned it to be a greater horseshoe bat and wondered if the information would be of use. Now it's not without reason that many of our birds and mammals are ringed and tagged in such enormous numbers, and there's no doubt that a tag is a personal identification and from it we can obtain information about longevity, for instance, and in some cases the distance and duration of migration. So it proved with Bat E3174.

The number and location of the find were passed to the office of the undoubted Batman of Britain, Dr Bob Stebbings, at the Institute of Terrestrial Ecology (Monks Wood Experimental Station, Abbots Ripton, Huntington, PE17 2LS). The reply came back within a very few days. Apparently E3174, a first-year female greater horseshoe bat, had been tagged in Cheddar in January 1978, recaught in the same cave three months later and found again in the famous Gough's Cave, Cheddar, at the end of October 1979. Here it was finding its final resting place when it was more than six years old. Thanks to the tag, we came up with quite a lot of information about E3174. Anyone finding a dead bat should examine it to see if it has a numbered tag and if so pass on the information to the Institute of Terrestrial Ecology.

Bat E3174 led to further contacts between that church and the Nature Conservancy Council (NCC) for, like many of our ancient churches, the church needed a new roof and the finder of E3174 was rightly concerned that bats might be disturbed once the scaffolding went up and the tiles came down and insecticides were sprayed into old timbers to kill off the deathwatch beetle infesting the roof. This is something that all parochial church councils must do before any work is carried out in a church in those places where bats may be roosting or breeding for this little mammal enjoys the greatest protection in law of any species in our countryside. 'Do not disturb' is but one of the strictures. We must not handle them, ring them (without a licence), photograph them (except on the wing), block up their entrance holes, damage or destroy their roosting buildings.

If any work is contemplated then the NCC will advise on whether the work should be done and if so the time of year when it may be done, and as far as the treatment of timbers goes then the Council will suggest the safe chemicals and methods to be used. If everyone observes the letter of the law (The Wildlife and Countryside Act) then long may we have bats in the belfry.

One bat that appeared on my doorstep with no identification card was in a shoe-box and had been found in a downstairs cloakroom, having managed to find its way through a tiny gap in the roof-light. 'What shall we do with it?' Keep it in a dark spot and then release it at dusk was my suggestion. A wire-mesh frame had been placed over the box and on top of this thick towelling. When the light began to fade that evening, we took the box and carefully lifted the blackout curtain and there was the small pipistrelle hanging upside down in the statutory bat position from the wire of the frame. Carefully lifting out the frame there was a couple of seconds pause, long enough for a flash photograph (I broke the law) and away it went into the evening sky. It has not reappeared in the cloakroom since that day much to the relief of some members of the family who, despite my public relations work on behalf of bats, still think of them unfavourably. It's a shame that bats have such a bad image so the more we can do on their behalf the better. They do not suck human blood nor do they tangle themselves in human hair nor are their droppings in the loft nasty and smelly – on the contrary, bat droppings make for better loft insulation!

There is one insulation still sought by many, particularly the ladies, that is a direct throwback to the first day in our ancient history when man the hunter killed his first wild animal and found its skin kept the winter chills out of his bones – animal fur. Today we don't need to go to such extremes to keep warm, and more and more people agree that a good fur looks much better on the animal for which it was intended. I remember one lady who was particularly proud of her leopard or cheetah fur who didn't get admiration from me for the garment. I hope I was diplomatic, although I've never been one to mince words. On reflection she must have been let off lightly for there was even greater pride in her voice when a few weeks later she told me she had sold the fur! It would be interesting to find whoever is wearing it now just to carry on the battle.

There is still a market for furs, furs taken from wild animals in our own countryside. The fox is a case in point and the destination for these furs is apparently the Continent where foxes are less numerous having been slaughtered over the years in the battle against rabies. In some years a fox skin in good condition can fetch anything up to £30, foxes caught in the winter months when the fur is thickest just before the mating season.

'Yer Derek, what should I do with this tag then?' So went the opening of a conversation with one chap I know whose knowledge of the countryside is strongly traditional. He keeps poultry: if a fox finds and kills his fowls or ducks he goes to war on the fox. What he handed me was a numbered tag taken from the ear of a fox he'd trapped near his livestock. It so happened that the origin of this tag was known. Dr Stephen Harris at the University of Bristol is engaged on a mammoth survey of the urban fox and in Bristol he has the ideal study area since the city seems to have a goodly population of them. He tags the ears of the animals, often when a litter of cubs is found under a garden shed or in a derelict building.

There was but one thing to do: put zoologist and trapper in touch with each other for the information the tag gave was important. It told how long the fox had lived, how far it had travelled out of the city from the day it was tagged and it was also worth a £5 note to the finder! He was patently pleased with the bounty that had come his way and several more tags from the ears of foxes changed hands in this way as did the agreed £5. I got the feeling that my country friend viewed trapping foxes on the outskirts of Bristol with renewed enthusiasm, particularly when we remember it was not just the case of the £5 notes but also that the skins of all these foxes were parcelled up and sent to an address in Cornwall where the dealer was paying up to six times the tag fee for a good skin! Ah well, when rabies reaches our shores foxes will be public enemy number one so the more we can learn about them now, especially in an urban environment, the better. For make no mistake about it, *all* foxes will have to be killed should rabies come across the channel and there will be none more difficult to deal with than those living under garden sheds in towns and cities and feeding right royally from our dustbins. Whatever method of control is used, whether poison or trapping, many domestic pets which wander freely at night will come to grief as well. Gassing would be impracticable in the towns for the city fox doesn't need to dig an earth as he does in the countryside. I hope pet owners will heed the gentle warning.

The snows of winter bring the greatest numbers of callers both on the telephone and at the front door, enquiring particularly about unusual birds that find refuge and food around the bird tables. I really needed a tape recording last winter describing redwings and fieldfares. Virtually every enquiry concerned birds that looked like thrushes but had a flash of red about them or big grey birds, all eating a variety of berries in the garden!

This was not difficult, but now and again comes the unexpected in the cold snows of winter. One neighbour reported a bird that can only have been a snipe probing about on a clear section of his lawn – Out with the books. 'That's the one!' As for blackcaps we seem to have had an invasion of them and patience was needed in explaining that the female of the species has a chestnut rather than a black cap. It was all very encouraging, though, that confined to the warmth of their homes villagers noticed that there was something *different* in the garden when probably in other times they wouldn't know the difference between a starling and a blackbird.

91

Matters of identification are usually pretty simple with the help of the right reference books when I can't come up with an immediate answer, but 'What shall we do with this baby bird that has fallen out of its nest?' is not quite so easy. My usual advice is shut up the cat for twenty-four hours and leave the fledgling where it is so that the parent can find it. That, of course, is a generalisation and fails when a young house martin is presented to you by a worried youngster. If it's well feathered the chances are that the first rule will suffice, but if it's a bald babe then you have trouble. Some would devote themselves to feeding it every time it gaped with insects caught from the kitchen window but that supply can never be enough. Just count the number of times the parent birds return to the nest with food in any hour and you will realise how much fodder the young need. No, it's a job best left to the parents and if it's possible to return the fledgling to the nest so much the better. If the whole nest has collapsed and you have a family of baldies on your hands try fixing a small box under the eaves – nails or strong adhesive tape will do the trick – and return the casualties to their new habitat. The parents will take over again and the exertion of putting up a ladder will be much less in the long run than devoting yourself to a wet-nurse role that could run into a couple of weeks!

Bird problems don't always come in small parcels. 'There are a couple of swans in the creek, covered in oil. What shall we do?' There was no way I was going to take out a boat and try to rescue them. This is the job for the experts, and in such cases there is always someone who knows what to do or where to get in touch with the best expert. There may be an RSPCA sanctuary in the locality; there may be a vet who specialises in oiled or injured birds; the RSPB could have a local contact; the police often have a telephone number for such emergencies; and the local office of the County Naturalists Trust will certainly be able to point in the right direction. If the distress of a bird causes you distress, keep trying until you find someone who can help.

I wonder if Hitchcock was responsible with his graphic film, but without doubt there are people around who unashamedly confess that they cannot touch birds. Show them a recently shot cock pheasant and they'll run a mile, but put the same bird, plucked, dressed and tenderly cooked on the table for sunday lunch and the fear disappears! How would they have coped in the countryside when the daily round of collecting eggs often meant gently putting your hand under those beautifully soft, downy breast feathers to collect eggs laid by other hens earlier, or taking a broody hen off her clutch of eggs so that she could eat, drink and carry out the usual bodily functions.

One of the village problems I've had to face is removing birds that had found themselves inside a house; starlings are common culprits, having fallen down a chimney stack. Starlings are noisy, aggressive birds with beaks of rapier-like quality and of very little sense! Inside a lounge they make dashes for freedom against walls, furniture and windows, invariably injuring themselves in the process and leaving blood all over the place. Grab them, holding them with folded wings in your hand with the thumb and forefinger as close to the head as possible. That beak is a dangerous weapon.

Moths are another matter. Never a summer goes by without a matchbox turning up at my front door with a beautiful hawk moth inside. Of all insects, these are my favourites. They're big, colourful and finely adapted to survive with warning flashes on the wing in some cases, camouflage in others. Their caterpillars are not so easy to identify, apart possibly from the elephant hawk moth for it is the caterpillar that gave the insect its name. That head elongates into the shape of a minute elephant trunk, and I awarded yet another accolade to my own garden on finding one such caterpillar happily chomping away at the leaves on a fuchsia. (This is one of its food plants but if you find one and want to follow it through its life-cycle willow herb leaves would be better.) Lovely caterpillars, lovely insects.

My doorbell rang again one day and there was Dave who regularly passes by on his bike in summer months to and from work. This day he had in his hand the standard plastic lunch-box. Inside, though, were no sandwiches but a large caterpillar, and we sat on the lawn browsing through the books trying to track down this beast with a reddish face, a body tinging to purple and two red whip-like lashes on a forked tail. It just had to be the larva of a puss moth yet the colour seemed just that shade too dark. Just before pupating the larva takes on this deeper purple hue. Dave, being the keen amateur naturalist that he is, was going to provide the necessary fodder of willow or poplar leaves just in case the caterpillar needed more food before it took that fascinating next step in its life-cycle cocooned in silken safety until emerging come spring into a soft, fluffy 'pussy' of a moth.

Thus my house is an information post where interested amateur naturalists have been able to swap notes with another of the same ilk and between us have sorted out the odd knotty problem. In a way it's possible to cheat a little through the facility of that modern device hated by many, the telephone answering machine. Thus I'm able to play back the anxious query and ponder on it before returning the call to the enquirer. The considered opinion always takes preference over the snap decision; but this is not always necessary, of course, like the recent mild winter enquiry which I found on the tape. 'Mr Jones, there's a bird singing outside my house during the night. It starts at about 1am and goes on for hours. It's a lovely song. I've recorded it and I wonder if you would be interested.' I'm always interested and the return call produced the vital missing piece of information: there was a street light close to the house. The inevitable robin was staking out an early claim on a December night for the territory it had picked out for spring days, for a mate and young and the beginning of new life.

My home, too, has taken on the air of a repository housing the strangest of items. Only recently I was given a large dried pod all of six inches long, a couple of inches wide, with a rattle of seeds inside (or maybe dried and very dead parasites). It is coloured with age, or the smoke of cigars or it may have been varnished! It has been around for years and in this case something of its history is known: it was given by a visiting dignitary from an African state to the secretary of a Lord Mayor. I think it's probably a mango, but then it could be almost anything.

Natural history is always a challenge: a detective story in many cases that needs the Sherlock Holmes magnifying glass, an enquiring mind that never accepts the obvious and the ability to put yourself in the situation of the culprit when the deed was done!

There's one mystery that still worries me, although there is a possible solution. To go back to the detection idea, the M.O. leaves no doubt that perhaps after all an innocent party is being blamed. Blame is hardly the right word since there has been no actual crime.

Situation: the village churchyard.

Evidence: activity of a badger and its distinctive latrines confirmed by the discovery of a run into the churchyard over a boundary wall as well as tracks.

Further clues: snuffle marks in the close mown grass suggesting brock has been finding worms.

Time: early winter when the berries on the yew trees have either fallen naturally or have been dropped by the wasteful mistle thrushes covering the path from lychgate to church door with a sticky red and slippery carpet.

Problem: why should the badger latrine be filled with the yew berries, berries that patently hadn't passed through the animal's digestive system but had been vomited?!

Conclusion: yew is poisonous, both the foliage to farm animals and the berries to humans. On the other hand, it is not poisonous to the thrushes who digest the flesh of the berry and excrete the seed, the poisonous part. So was this a badger in the process of learning what is and what is not to be eaten? From the piles of berries in the latrine scrapes it was taking a long time to learn the lesson, and strangely once the crop of berries had fallen from the new trees the badger disappeared too. One of those mysteries and I only hope my detective work has closed that particular file.

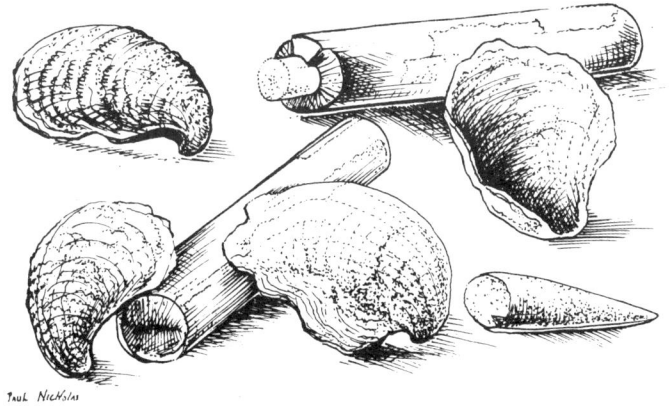

Paul Nicholas

9
SMELLS, SOUNDS AND BEING SEEN

As the very first BBC station to provide me with work was set in the grounds of a sewage works it's not really surprising that smells remain firmly in my memory. Anyone who walked the bomb-ruined streets of Hamburg in Germany after the Second World War could not fail to notice the stench of death that stalked and dogged one's footsteps. Black crosses painted on the rubble of a building indicated that bodies hadn't been recovered. Those crosses were unnecessary to tell of the evil and waste of war, of life that had been extinguished.

Many countryside smells may tell *our* nostrils that there is a nastiness or rot, but to some animals these smells have a very different message, be it to mark a territory, attract a mate or pursuade an insect to land and help in the complicated job of future life. Or perhaps the smell spells a warning, a defence mechanism.

Some animals will take advantage of the armoury of others. Take anting. Most people have seen birds on the lawn in high summer looking as scruffy and tattered as a mongrel dog; blackbirds, for instance, with feathers spread out like a fan, pecking around the soil or grass and making their plumage even more untidy. They are picking up ants and using the insect's defence mechanism, formic acid, to clean their own skin and feathers. Body cleanliness comes a very close second to food in birdlife survival. But have you ever smelt formic acid squirted by an ant? If you're ever in woodland or open heathland near woods and find a vibrating nest of wood ants, try this experiment encountered on a *Living World* trip to the Peak District. It's best tried on a sunny day. Pass one hand, palm downwards, over the top of the nest. The shadow made by your hand will stimulate the ants into defending their territory by bombarding the shadow above them with formic acid. If you've a sensitive skin this will produce a slight irritation and, as for the smell, you'll never forget it!

Never forgotten either is probably the foulest smell there is in the countryside and one associated with late hot summer days and bracken and high banks and deep woodlands. Some describe it as rotting flesh: the smell of the strange fungus, the stinkhorn. The scientific name describes it precisely, *Phallus impudicus!* The smell of rotting flesh attracts flies in some numbers, as they would be attracted to a decaying carcass, and in that attraction lies the fungal success. Flies come to it, walk over its surface and take away with them some of the spores to lose them elsewhere. Survival of the species! Life complicated on one hand but delightfully simple on the other.

The derogatory term 'stinking like a polecat' is used commonly enough but never having had a close encounter with a true polecat I can't vouch for its smell, although since it used to be known as the foul marten there is undoubted truth in the simile. Some ferrets are very nearly polecats and they really do have, to us, an anti-social odour. Yet they make useful pets and not a little country humour for those prepared to let them wander loose down a trouser leg!

For an after-shave lotion that really lingers and keeps everyone at bay, try handling a grass snake. In fact, you wouldn't need to distribute the perfume because it spreads and permeates of its own accord and out-stinks a skunk. Here is the animal's secondary defence mechanism (the other is shamming death) and I can vouch for it being one of the most clinging perfumes known. Perhaps there is one more: a fishy, oil mixture shot with astonishing accuracy by some seabirds at any human intruder during the nesting season. Rock climbers tend to come home with clothing best consigned to the incinerator, likewise naturalists finding themselves in the middle of skua colonies on the Shetlands! I know.

Smells are what you get used to and familiarity breeds oblivion. Farmer friends express surprise when one remarks that the silage fed that day to their herd of cows seems rather ripe. They have become so used to the smell that it no longer has any impact. It is part of the background. Having said that, I cannot understand why the scent marks left by a dog fox are not noticed by people who have no regular contact with the animal. To me that musty smell is unmistakable although it passes with maybe half a step on your walk. It is confined to a very small area and my nose picks it up straight away. Maybe the reason more walkers don't get the niff is that it is just 'another country smell' like a damp autumn woodland littered with the decaying leaves of the year. Yet in a forest floor there is a symphony of smells, each having an individual character, each having a meaning.

Radio and television cannot transmit scent, but in terms of sound transmission there have been enormous advances, stereo being a case in point. We tried to produce radio nature trails in stereo when the equipment was much more cumbersome than it is today and required the attentions of a couple of engineers to add to the crowd. Crowds are anathema to nature trails. Just imagine the situation where an interesting bird has been spotted in a nearby tree. Let's record! We have to set up two microphones to get the true stereo effect from the two speakers. 'Now which side were you last time, Derek? Now let's try it for level.' By which time the bird in the tree has long since disappeared. Those were early experiments with only limited success and limited appeal. Today equipment has advanced and we've tried a few binoral broadcasts.

For the best effect this should be heard with stereo headphones with the result that one's head seems to be surrounded by the recorded sounds. Oddly enough, in recording a programme at the Wildfowl Trust at Slimbridge the producer, Michael Bright, used a microphone system that looked for all the world exactly like a human head. It was a plastic replica with two microphones inside in the position of the human ears, but not visible. I can't imagine what the crowds of people wandering around Slimbridge that day among the hosts of ducks and geese could have thought we were doing, seeing otherwise normal chaps, Mike Ounsted, the Trust curator, and myself talking with a plastic head between us. And a plastic head with a woolly bonnet to boot! The bonnet was functional: not to keep out the cold, just the draught! It acted as a shield to lessen the effect of the wind on the microphones. What was even more surprising was the reaction of the Slimbridge collection. Goslings of the Hawaiian geese (nenes, the endangered species now being reintroduced to their one-time native habitats) were nothing short of inquisitive. The binoral head placed inside their pen had the effect of making them come close and make beautiful contact calls all of which our recording captured. It was a salutary lesson, though, and one of the reasons for the decline of the goose in the wild: their lack of fear.

Radio nature trails have given me years of pleasure and hours of discomfort. A classic case of the latter was in Yorkshire, wading through floods to reach a hide and spend some hours watching the birds on the water-inundated fields near the banks of a river. I thought I was well prepared, jumping out of the car, opening the boot and donning the winter clothing necessary for such a day: good thick waterproof and windproof jacket, waterproof trousers, gloves and finally the statutory Wellington boots. We advanced towards the objective on the other side of the floodwater. The first step told the horrible truth – a large leak! By the time we reached the hide with Michael Clegg, the leak had collected a bootful of extremely cold water and it's no pleasure to sit for four hours in a cold hide with visions of frostbite invading the right foot. Still, the end result was worth it.

That was a pleasure in a way. Others are just as memorable if less taxing. Like watching at close quarters, say ten yards distance, a seal devouring a large fish in the sea off the Isles of Scilly. Throwing it around like a Wimbledon champion tossing the ball high in the air before playing an ace. The seal did just that, catching its meal after tossing it in the air and taking another bite. Or wandering through the clay workings of a brick company and finding fossils of animals rather like cuttlefish where today the sea is many miles away. (Belemnites are the fossils often found with Devil's Toenails, fossilised molluscs.)

Some of our *Living World* contributors had a regular and enthusiastic following. One was Dog. We made many trips out to Little England beyond Wales, that is Pembrokeshire, to meet that delightful and enthusiastic naturalist, John Barrett, at his home at Dale. Dog belonged to John, or rather they belonged to each other, and I use the past tense since Dog has taken his last rush across the mud flats, his last scamper around the headland. John's nature trails were never very taxing on the stamina. Some required little more than a 20yd scramble down through the rocks to the beach; others might have been stretched to the whole distance between the high and low tide marks, and occasionally we even got our feet wet in the water! But at every yard with John there was something different to enthuse over as differing life forms find their niches at different levels on the beach or foreshore. There was usually the added advantage of not being more than hailing distance from his house so that should the weather turn

101

nasty shelter was not far away. One such day will always stay with me. As we looked at limpets, perhaps we even listened to them grazing over a rock surface, there was a distant rumbling which had the continuity of a barrage. 'Oh, nothing to worry about,' said John, 'only the tanks on manoeuvres at the range at Castle Martin.' The barrage came ominously closer which suggested that full-scale war had broken out! Then the heavens opened. A thunderstorm! Some tank range! A bark from Dog sent us homewards. Dog made some canine remark in all those programmes until the day came when we had to do without his company and his bark. That absence was noticed by listeners who wrote to ask why Dog didn't appear in that particular broadcast. Loyalty indeed.

Interviewing John is the broadcaster's dream. One pertinent question launches him into a full dissertation with all the facts one could wish for. Others are not so easy. The art of interviewing should be quite simply asking questions which inspire the interviewee to answer in a way that gives all the facts (with politicians the technique is somewhat different). The bad interview goes something like this:

Interviewer: Now you've been shipwrecked, Mr Crusoe, on an uninhabited island for twenty-seven days with no fresh water and you had to get liquid intake from wild fruits and you made a fishing line and caught fish to eat and you lost two stone in weight because of the poor food and were rescued by a passing yachtsman who saw the fire you had managed to light despite having no matches. And the parrot you had befriended refused to leave saying 'Get lost sailor'. Is that so?

Mr Crusoe: Yes.

A slight exaggeration perhaps but an example of how not to conduct an interview. The other habit that seems to have crept into common usage is to put a *statement* rather than a question, and to turn it into an enquiry by the phrase: 'Do you have anything to say to that?'

If only some people would remember that the best way to

get the information wanted is to begin your question with words starting with the letter 'W', we would have much more professional broadcasting. 'What', 'why', 'where' and 'when' are not bad starters and usually have the effect of getting away from dull monosyllabic replies. The man, or woman, holding the microphone should always remember the pecking order. The listeners want to hear the person being interviewed, and those with the questions should be so secondary as to be almost invisible. There are exceptions, of course, as in the case of politicians and others who are deliberately evasive. And then there are those who take advantage of the microphone being thrust under their noses and set about a diatribe which has nothing to do with the reason the interview is taking place and instead use the broadcast to get across their pet theories or doctrines. They deserve the hardest interview where no quarter is given.

I didn't rate much for my chances of getting a good interview when a studio in the bowels of Broadcasting House in London had a gremlin producing strange noises from behind the whole length of one wall and a 'Goon' spent the next ten minutes crawling on all fours around the studio floor apparently trying to find the origins of the extraneous sounds! But then talking to Spike Milligan is like taking on a porcupine in unarmed combat. This was for a long-running series *Sounds Natural* in which personalities from show business and elsewhere let us into the secrets of their passion for wildlife. Producer John Burton illustrated their anecdotes with some of the thousands of recordings from the BBC Natural History Sound Library. In fairness to Spike, once he had got the other sounds out of his system, we had as sensible a conversation as one could expect from such a volatile and funny character.

Some of the people who took part in that series were not as unpredictable as Mr Milligan, but Eric Morecambe came a very close second. What the series showed, though, was that personalities prominent on the world stage were very concerned and knowledgeable about the wildlife of the world. Bill Oddie, for instance, is a renowned 'twitcher' and possesses an encyclopaedic mind on scientific ornithology; Lord Home of the Hirsel had to confine his bird-watching to the confines of the garden of Number 10 when he was Prime Minister until he could return to his beloved Scotland; Bill Travers and Virginia McKenna are now equally well known in the world of conservation; these and many more were a joy to talk to and I hope a listening pleasure. There were just two I was apprehensive of meeting: one was a Royal Prince, the other had no peer in show business.

Bing Crosby was a charmer. He was in Britain shortly before his death, on a tour that was a typical Crosby itinerary with golf at the top of the priorities; yet he was gentleman enough to agree to take part in *Sounds Natural*. The family entourage was staying in a house in Holland Park and to our surprise Bing agreed to meet us one morning during his visit. There's no doubt about it, had he not been born American he would have been British. Was this a slight jealousy of the origins of his long-time partner and jokester Bob Hope?

A 'man', who presumably went with the highly expensive accommodation, met the BBC team at the door and ushered us in with the deference that made one feel an intruder. Bing eventually joined us by which time the recording machine had been checked and all was set for 'go'. Explanations of the programme over in the shortest possible time (was he anxious to reach the first tee at Wentworth?), we sat and started to chat about his interest in wildlife and conservation. It soon became obvious that Crosby was not only a golfer but a hunter as well. That is to use the American definition, meaning that he was a shooting man! But shooting laws, or hunting laws in their terms, have a strong concern for the bag size that may be taken by the gun. The chat went on, taking in American birds that have featured in his songs. Not only did he know what a whippoorwill was but he could whistle its song! Cue for record for those who knew their Crosby discographies. But what impressed me more than anything else was his happiness to talk to a chap so patently involved in natural history and after the first preambles so much at ease.

Two hours after the recording machine was switched on at the start of our conversation, we were still chatting away until we were conscious of Gary, son of Bing, then an amateur golfer of some standing, and now on the Pro circuit, hovering for the second or third time. It was two hours of absolute joy and I can only be happy that we met and talked. I don't very often shed tears but his passing left a gap in my life. Bing wasn't just an entertainer, he was an institution despite the mud that has been dragged up since his death. I just wish that after our meeting on that morning in London I could have joined him on the first tee and played a round of golf, not concerned with a winner or loser, but two men on the same wavelength enjoying each other's company. Had that happened he might have been reminded of our first encounter when as a callow youth I was in the Paris Cinema in Lower Regent Street for a broadcast by Bing singing with George Melachrino conducting the British Band of the Allied Expeditionary Forces. That was a moment too for my girlfriend of the day who is probably still remembering it. Bing is dead, but as Alistair Cooke said in talking of Duke Ellington 'I don't have to believe it.'

Being served coffee from solid silver pots and cream jugs by a liveried servant wearing speckless white gloves doesn't very often happen to broadcasters. Mind you, this was rather special, and happened at the Royal Dutch Palace at Soestdijk where His Royal Highness Prince Bernhardt had agreed to record a *Sounds Natural* programme. We sat in his study surrounded by an amazing collection of hunting trophies which didn't augur well in conservation terms, yet we should not forget that many of the voices raised in defence of world wildlife today began their interest by following the inbred human trait of 'man the hunter'. Is it any different from the present-day ornithologist whose

105

interest was awakened by collecting birds' eggs? That's how I started and I'm the rule rather than the exception.

There is a sheer fear in the mind of a broadcaster sitting in a royal study awaiting a prince of a royal household. Remember the rules. Address him once with 'Your Royal Highness' and thereafter a polite 'Sir' at infrequent intervals will be all that's necessary. It was a most interesting meeting for as soon as we started the recording I sensed that he was just as nervous as me! It wasn't that he didn't understand the questions for his English was near perfect. I can only assume on analysing the situation in retrospect that the apprehension may have arisen in case the interview veered off the subject of natural history. Within five minutes the concern on both sides of the microphone disappeared and we got on famously talking of his work for the World Wildlife Fund and his travels. He couldn't have been more charming and set no limit on the time we spent with him with his collection of pipes and trophies in that splendidly manly royal study.

Does a Seigneur rate as a royal personage? If the description covers the feudal ruler of a small island 'kingdom' then he must, and once on the tiny Channel Island of Sark true royalty was also involved. When La Dame de Sark died the title passed to her grandson Michael Beaumont, a boffin with the British Aircraft Corporation in Bristol. It was decided to make a film following Michael and his charming wife Diana from their home to the island that heredity ruled should be theirs. It was a tremendous upheaval, made all the more difficult in that, shortly after their arrival, Sark was to have a royal visit by Queen Elizabeth, The Queen Mother.

The only way for ordinary beings, and Seigneurs too for that matter, to reach Sark is by boat from Guernsey and our film crew duly loaded up onto the cargo boat aptly named *La Dame de Sark*. Sark has some wonderful laws concerning keeping pigeons, breeding bitches and motor vehicles: there are no cars! Horse-drawn carriages and tractors, yes, but that is the limit. In her day La Dame had a special law put through to allow her to have mobility in an invalid carriage. So what was a film crew to do? Hiring a tractor and trailer was the answer but on making enquiries and starting negotiations (haggling it's called) we came to the conclusion that the budget wouldn't stretch that far. (We discovered that a film crew from London had preceded us by a week and had thrown paper money around like confetti, so the going rate was somewhat high.) The budget, our producer Mike Fitzgerald decided, would stretch to bicycles! So be it. A tractor and trailer was hired to take us up the steep harbour hill to the top of the island and our hotel and from then, apart from one day when we had to have a tractor to move lighting gear, we travelled in the saddle. It must have been the first time that a BBC film crew went from location to location with a convoy of six bikes. Each had a basket on the handlebars so one bike carried, precariously, the camera, tripod (large) for same strapped to a crossbar; tripod (small) in another basket; recording machine, another very expensive piece of equipment, in yet another basket; microphones and cables, clapper board, hand-held lights and a pile of bits and pieces spread around the other bikes where they could be fitted in. The dusty roads on Sark are something lower than class B and some of the crew had to refresh their memories about controlling a two-wheeled velocipede – with bruising disasters initially! We had rehearsals first *without* the film gear, of course!

Even as we filmed during the few days of our stay, preparations were still not complete for the royal occasion, and should you ever visit La Seigneurie where Michael and Diana live take a look at the box hedges. They were clipped into shape for the big day on Sark by members of the BBC film crew when not needed for filming duty!

The law had been suitably amended by the island parliament, the Chief Pleas, to allow landing by a helicopter of the Queen's Flight and the royal visit got under way – followed by the BBC bikes. At the end of the tour, tea was taken in La Seigneurie and, quite against the rules, a radio mic was hidden in the foliage around the front door so that we could hear the farewells between the feudal lord and his royal guest before Her Majesty entered the horse-drawn carriage taking her back to the football pitch, the makeshift landing ground for the helicopter. The Queen Mother was obviously well aware of the activities of this off-beat film crew, and I shall always treasure her final wave as the carriage swung out of the drive: her wave and smile direct to camera were timed to perfection.

With the last shots safely on film with the departure of the helicopter, the six bikes replaced the royal carriage outside La Seigneurie and a relaxed team repaired inside the house, where we had been welcome for several days, for tea. There were still some scones and small sandwiches left (I seem to remember there had been a disaster with the first scone baking) and time to relax with The Seigneur and Mrs Beaumont and reflect on how the great day had gone. The unanimous decision was that it had been a success, as one of our crew disappeared once more to make another pot of tea. By that time we knew our way around the kitchen as well as the Beaumonts. Making a film with them and about them hadn't been a job of work, it had been fun.

My one regret about Sark is that we have never made a natural history radio programme there for it is crying out to be investigated by *The Living World*. When riding around Sark on your bicycle you occasionally have to swerve to one side to avoid a song thrush using a convenient stone on the track as an anvil to crack a snail from its shell; when you swim in the evening in a hotel pool your only company will be swallows taking insects or a sip of water from the pool's surface around your ears; when the light fades to dusk bats flit to and fro from the caves and tunnels left behind from German defence works. It's some place. As if that isn't enough, the flowers in the small fields remind you of ancient meadowland now so sadly missing from our mainland landscape. Sark would come close to Paradise in my book.

Back in Bristol. Eventually, after the long drawn-out
business of processing and editing the film, came the time to
write further commentary before the final dubbing. Film
commentaries are so specialised as to drive the most
competent word-mongers to distraction. There is so little
time. Film editors and directors get carried away with the
artistry of the shots and forget that some poor word-man
has to be perhaps poetic, perhaps informative, preferably
both, in the spaces. In other words, the picture takes over,
and in some cutting rooms the commentator is used in a less
than secondary role. Indeed, in some situations where the
editor and director like a sequence pictorially, they exepct
the commentator to cover it with words of wisdom when in
fact there's absolutely nothing to say. When in doubt use
music. So the problems of making a flowing commentary
can be near impossible. This was not the case in the Sark
film since we all worked together as a team. The bikes were
ghosts haunting even the cutting room.

Radio has always been my forte with few temptations put
my way to expose myself (if you'll pardon the expression) to
the screen. There was one series, though, that gave me
enormous pleasure as well as new insight into the
Westcountry, the series *Day Out* for the BBC West Region
in Bristol, and thus seen in a relatively small part of the
country. Some of the many programmes were repeated on
BBC 2 and seen by a wider audience, and a further series
was taken on board by the Midlands Region in
Birmingham. The formula was simple: walk around a town,
village or locality pointing out the architectural features, the
history of the buildings, the strange stories. And didn't we
find some beauties. Like a pub at Lacock in Wiltshire where
in the bar there is an old spit over an open fireplace
connected to a treadmill, in which (away from the heat) a
dog was placed in days gone by. The dog walked, the spit
turned, and the joint was 'done to a turn'! But for the
purposes of the film we did without a dog. Like finding a
man who collects from the River Severn enough coal to fuel

109

his fire through the entire winter. Like sitting locked in the stocks at Painswick. But these walks in the Westcountry have been described elsewhere (*Day Out*, Series One to Four with Derek Jones and Gwyn Richards, published by Abson Books).

Some television personalities bask in the sunshine of self-importance and *want* to be recognised as they walk down a street or make some insignificant purchase in a store. Others frequently exposed to the 'cinema in every home' try to walk through their part as if it were nothing more than doing a job of work like a road-sweeper or a dustman. And in the final analysis that is all it is – doing a job of work – though some people, inside and outside the business, clothe it in the glamour of show business. Being seen on television is regarded as bordering on stardom. How many reporters have been seen in locations ranging from the touchline of a local football match to the wrecked background of a bomb outrage, from interviews with union officials to those with ministers of state, with a backcloth of waving idiots anxious to be seen on the box? The film or television camera attracts them like flies, and sadly the day will never come when the man trying to do his job will be free of such stupid and wasteful intrusion. With film, then there's another few quids worth of stock to be thrown in the bin. With video cameras, it's merely a waste of time. I once felt moved to remonstrate with a youngster who, seeing our camera in the city of Bristol, went through the all too familiar antics of arm-waving and grotesque grimaces right into the camera lens as I walked and talked trying desperately to remember my words for a sequence in *Day Out*.

The 'take' was of course ruined by his anxiety to get on the 'box'. In anger, he was given what would probably be the cause of a school enquiry had it happened in the classroom but I would consider nothing more than a bit of a roasting. When he apologised, in halting English, it became clear that he was a German visitor to the city. His mother, standing apart, took no interest. Perhaps, later, she gave him more of a roasting.

Sometimes the intrusion is not premeditated. There was a day filming in Gloucestershire when, having learnt my lines, I had to walk up a steep narrow street explaining that the houses on my right used to be the houses of weavers. It was not an easy location for there were shadows which I had to negotiate; the slope was lung-emptying; it had to be timed without a passing car; the words had to be right – or at least words to that effect. I was in full flow when a lady came out of a gate to my right and buttonholed me as the words came mercifully to mind. Interrupting the 'take', she invited me to come and look into her garden and see the view across the valley. Who could 'roast' such an intrusion? I patiently explained that when we had finished filming the sequence I would gladly come and look at her garden – and we did. All concerned were more than delighted for not only did she feed the entire crew with coffee and scones but she had an eye for the picture: the view from her garden featured in the film!

The day after appearing on the screen it's advisable to hide. Shy and retiring, and still looking on television as just another job, I am embarrassed by recognition. Is it always so certain? Playing it cool while still recognising I am an unpaid BBC public relations man can be fun. Complete strangers buttonhole me. 'Excuse me, but I'm sure I know you. Surely it was Budleigh Salterton in, let's see, 1977 wasn't it?' 'I don't think so' is my reply. Undeterred he goes on 'Don't tell me, it'll come back to me in a minute – not Budleigh Salterton? It must have been somewhere in Devon where we always spend our holidays. No, *you* tell *me*.' I then gently suggest that he may have been watching BBC 1 last evening, and that is a true situation. This can only happen to those who appear but infrequently on the box and perhaps that is our refuge – we don't have to wear the false beard and dark glasses.

You get to recognise those 'I've seen you before'

thought-bubbles. Standing one evening in the snug of my local pub, two characters came in through the door and one glance was enough to see the balloons sprouting from their heads like methane bursting from a bog. Two pints ordered and in hand, one of them could no longer keep his thoughts to himself. He was terribly polite. 'Excuse me, sir,' he said with the deference due to a duke. 'But you bear a striking resemblance to someone I've seen on television.' Containing my mirth, my quickly studied reply took the heat and further conversation out of the situation. 'Yes,' I said, 'I'm often told that.' With which I left. The barmaid then made the hastiest retreat she's ever made convulsed in girlish giggles. I'm told that after this meeting she told the customers the true identity of the chap who had just left the bar. Fun!

It's not so funny, though, on the other side of the coin. Front-men are always dispensable; they are just another item on the costing list of any production and despite what the public may think in placing them on pedestals, there comes a time when the front office makes a decision and they are rested in favour of another. I just wish that those sitting in that front office would remember that in taking on a presenter (what a ghastly word: let's get back to the more refined compère) they have made that person an indivisible part of their programme. So much so that the public regard it as *his* programme.

I wish, too, that they were recognised in the street and complimented upon on the programme, or that they had to parry the questions when another has been pushed up front. Questions like 'Why aren't you doing your programme?' This is the moment when the freelance needs nerves of steel. He may be flippant and suggest his vital statistics are not as attractive as they might be. But, being a pro, he'll brush it aside and still remember his unpaid role in the public relations business of radio and television. Mind you, as he walks away he'll grab his dark glasses and pray that he was as convincing as his performance on radio or television. It's a hard life, but it can be fun.

10
GAFFES AND BLOOMERS

It ill behoves anyone to criticise others without admitting first to some of his own bloomers, and let it be said that it is very easy in the heat of the moment of broadcasting to let the occasional slip show. Confessions!

I once killed someone off while introducing the Hamburg end of *Two Way Family Favourites* in the delightful company of Jean Metcalfe in London. Our end of the programme was scripted in the vaguest possible way since one had to be ready for the ad lib exchanges with Jean. I had got around to introducing a record by Turner Layton; I forget which one it was with the passing of time. He had been famous as a member of a duo, Layton and Johnson, and in introducing his solo record a little chord in my memory suddenly told me he was no longer with us. So, straight in with both feet! A record by the *late* Turner Layton. 'Oops', said Jean. And rescued me, bless her. It was, of course, his partner who was late, killed by a bomb on a

London Club. Carpet the next day – but the pile was pretty thick and soft. These are the sort of mistakes that teach you the trade where the maxim in the heat of the moment of ad lib informal broadcasting must be 'If in doubt, leave it out'.

'There's an old couple hard at it over there'. Oh yes, it was broadcast. It was a *Living World* programme at Dollis Hill in London, looking at the variety of birdlife in the built-up areas of the Metropolis. In vivid phrases, I set the scene, describing the topography of the hill on which we stood and pointing out that here was a large area of allotments, some well tended and others suffering from neglect, yet here on a chill autumn day was this old couple 'hard at it' – the best way I could describe the care and attention two pensioners were putting into their plot. As the words left my brain and came spouting forth, I was conscious out of the corner of my eye that the producer, Dilys Breese, was convulsing quietly. Then the penny dropped about my inept choice of phrase! The phrase, though, stayed in the programme.

Those, then, are some of my confessions. There may have been many more in the area where most clangers are dropped: the idiosyncratic pronunciation of some of our place names and surnames. The graveyard of many a broadcaster must be the Channel Islands with the peculiar local patios. One example is the surname Le Mesurier. Jerseymen give it the French touch but Guernseymen prefer a slight Anglicisation and it is Le Measurer! The pitfalls there are dark and deep and not to be explored by the unwary without the protection of several feet of armour plate.

Even one's own relations fire flak, as was brought home by my dear sister-in-law who hails from the north and took me to task about one of those place names that looks straightforward but is anything but. Alnwick. Look it up in the book, friend, you'll find it is 'Annick'. While you're at it, consult the book of words and check on that Glaswegian suburb Milngavie. You'll find 'Mawlgie'.

Plant names can also trap the unwary. One shrub – the cotoneaster – gives untold delight in the garden, spring, summer, autumn and winter, and yet it is repayed by mutilation at the mouths of those who should know better. Early spring honeybees flock to it in swarms as the tight insignificant flowers reluctantly open a little in the spring sunshine. Masses of berries formed through the summer and autumn give them a brighter, richer hue, matched by the changing colour of the foliage which can become as cherry-red as the fruit. In my own garden *Cotoneaster horizontalis* sprawls over the walls, giving in winter yet another joy as a cache of food for the birds spending the cold days with us. Yet, how is it that some people have a mental block about the name and by their pronunciation give the impression that it is a native of the Nile Delta or the fields of the Southern States of America that comes into flower immediately after Lent? Cotton Easter indeed! I've heard it dozens of times.

Right next to the wall-sprawl in the Jones garden is a rose: not a new-fangled, interbred type, but a good old-fashioned variety with a vigorous habit and a glorious scent, with flowers that shade through from salmon pink to creamy white, like the skin on the neck of a desirable, delectable nymph. Penelope by name. But one famous commentator who shall be nameless was taking us through a conducted tour of the Chelsea Flower Show when he came upon an absolute beauty of the standard at which that horticultural Mecca excels. He drew our attention to it. Pen-Elope, he said!

Classics among clangers must be the delightful spoonerisms that have been perpetrated by some of my distinguished colleagues, although a couple of them are so good that one can't help thinking that they are deliberate. It's rather like dear John Arlott's comment that the best ad libs are planned, such as his phrase 'that shot was so late it was almost posthumous'. He used it several times too!

What comes to mind are the ringing Oxford-accent tones of the announcer who told us 'We are now going over to the Bath Room at Pump' or, on another serious musical event,

'A recital now of mad songs and partrigals'. Classics indeed.

One such that didn't reach the air, although it did reach inside the studio door, occurred during the days of the Regional *Today* programme from the south and west. The commissionaires at the front reception desk are pillars of the establishment and well versed in 'the way things should be done'. Just after eight o'clock one morning a distinguished-looking gentleman turned up and was politely asked his name and his business. 'Darling', he replied, 'and a live interview in the Today programme'. With the bearing of a military policeman, he was led to Studio 7 and ushered in. He was announced by the commissionaire rather like a toastmaster would introduce speakers at a banquet. 'Mr Darling to see you, sir', he said. The faces of the producer and myself must have been a sight to see for, you've probably guessed, into the studio had come the Lord Darling, the then secretary of the Bath and West Society, it being Bath and West Show week. I can't help wondering what thoughts must have gone through the mind of our commissionaire when the first word he heard from a gentleman at that hour was darling! As I said, they didn't usually flinch in the face of adversity.

In these days, when so many programmes are recorded on tape, the razor blade rules; for wielded by the producer anything that doesn't work as it should can be excised. To my mind it makes for lazier broadcasting since every performer at the microphone knows in the back of the mind that any indiscretion, any error, any 'fluff' can be conjured away before it descends on the tender ears of the listeners. Give me the days when every broadcast was 'live'. The adrenalin flowed, the mistakes were fewer, the broadcasts had more edge.

Given that the razor blade and the tape can change the shape of the broadcast, we live with the system, sometimes gratefully. I got cold feet once after a recording in Cornwall with that splendid singer Frederick Harvey and one of those Cornish male voice choirs with voices so pure, deep and

116

resonant that to hear them induces a vibration right through the guts. Freddy and the choir had sung 'The Cobbler's Song' from *Chu Chin Chow* and, in the happy relaxed style of presentation that has always been my approach, I added a comment as the last echo came back from the rafters of the hall: 'Well that was a load of old cobblers'. The next day, I had second thoughts, even though the producer had made no contrary noises at the time. I made a 'phone call suggesting that it might be better to cut that remark. By this time the producer had fallen ill and the tape was in London ready for transmission. I still felt apprehensive and managed to contact a music department producer at Broadcasting House and he promised to get hold of the tape and the necessary razor blade. He was as good as his word and the phrase never reached the air. Today, of course, it wouldn't have mattered a jot, but then, in the sixties there was still a shadow of Reith hanging over anyone who appeared at the microphone.

One of our *Living World* contributors didn't even bother to use cockney rhyming slang to disguise his meaning. It was in Ireland on the estate of Lord Kilbracken. David Streeter was explaining about the medicinal uses in ancient times of the root of the early purple orchid and spoke of its once-believed aphrodisiac qualities. Culpeper in his *Complete Herbal and English Physician* wrote that it provoked 'lust exceedingly'. David was explaining that many of the ancient beliefs arose because of an association of shapes; in the case of the orchids their roots resembled male genital parts. John Kilbracken listened and then, after a short pause, remarked 'It sounds like a load of balls to me.' Back in Bristol, the producer exercised his editorial supervision and used the inevitable razor blade to cut out that particular indiscretion from the programme! Ah well, another one that got away.

My house must often echo these days into those of my neighbours several doors away when I hear a 'Beeb boob', particularly of Radio 4, and shout back to those who should know better. From the current news one may hear as many different deliveries of 'apartheid' as there are balls in a bad Jeff Thomson over. 'Meteorological' and 'veterinary' are a couple more that present problems. I've heard 'chasm' given the benefit of the shortened Charles with an 'm' added; Pas de Calais in many different ways; the composer San Saens has come out without anything!

It's the grammatical clanger, though, that really has me screaming. 'The government have decided . . .', 'The council have ordered . . .', 'At a meeting today Exmoor National Park Committee have allowed . . .', 'A group of tourists have left. . . .'. It's clear enough in the printed word. A committee, a council, a government, a group, is singular and the verb should be likewise. Prefaced by members of the committee or whatever, that is another matter, and the word 'have' becomes correct, but please, oh please, get it right. In such cases it is often the fault of the editor or sub-editor who has prepared a news bulletin and he or she should be given the appropriate rocket, but there are responsibilities that the man or woman at the microphone should shoulder personally. There is no excuse for the mistake. There are available splendid pronunciation guides produced by the BBC, widely on sale, and usually near to hand even in a BBC studio. If not, a direct call to the Pronunciation Unit in London will come up with an immediate answer, and there are regular circulations of recommended pronunciations of places and people in the news from distant parts. Mistakes will still be made, but Auntie, please, oh please, pull up your knickers.

11
OF FISH AND FISHERMEN

Have you ever tickled a trout? This is one of those country arts done with dexterity, tried by myself and failed. There was one of those meandering Welsh streams a crowd of us passed twice a day to and from New Radnor School, and before climbing the steep track over the Smatcher or coming down the homeward hillside the stream was a temptation few could resist on a hot summer day. In winter it wasn't given a second glance. A large boulder conveniently placed by some previous deluge enabled you to crawl on top of it out of sight of any fish that might be lurking underneath, and it was possible to stretch forward with sleeves pulled up over the elbows and gently, oh so gently, finger-search for fish. There was often one there, touchable, but as for flicking it out to gasp on dry land, never. In later years a small Somerset brook was known to give up its fish to a small red worm on the end of a hook and line but that wasn't sport, that was strictly for the pot.

Not so long ago viewers in the Westcountry will have seen a *Day Out* BBC television programme exploring the magnetic majesty of Exmoor and in particular the town at its gateway, Dulverton. In the film the presenter was seen being taught the basic points of casting for salmon and trout by the side of a stretch of the River Exe. The fact that neither salmon nor trout fell to the rod was immaterial. Fishing closely follows hunting as the recreation of the area. This was one way of reflecting the pursuits that draw holiday-makers there in their thousands and ensure that locals stay as locals as long as life-spans will allow. Knowing something of fishing, I didn't really expect even the stupidest of salmon or thickest of trout to give themselves up for the sake of a few television pictures. Fishing is a loner's game. Gather a crowd around, and salmon head for the shadows; and make no mistake, we had a bit of a crowd. One producer, one producer's assistant, one film cameraman, one assistant cameraman, one sound recordist, the water bailiff from the Carnarvon Arms Hotel, and me! Too many, as was proved later in the day when the bailiff returned to the hotel with two splendid salmon taken from that very piece of water where we had been filming earlier! There's the lesson about loners!

That television programme spurred me on to take up the sport far more seriously than in the past and, subscribing to the theory that if you want a job done properly, be it plumbing a house or building a brick wall, you go to the experts – I did just that.

It was back to the Carnarvon Arms for a few days' relaxation and a determination to get to grips with a pastime that provides countless millions with pleasure. Imagine a very hot afternoon in mid-summer when the grass around the hotel had lost its chlorophyll colour and gone to a shade much nearer desert sands. Three keen pupils lined up under the watchful eyes of the hotel manager, John Sharp, and Lance Nicholson, a local man who provides for every sporting need from his shop in the

120

town; what he doesn't know about fishing isn't worth knowing.

It soon became obvious that this so-called pleasurable pastime called for more than a little hard work. 'Rod back to the twelve o'clock position, pause, flick forward to ten o'clock. Let the line out through the left hand. Don't break your wrist. You're breaking your wrist! You're breaking your wrist again!' So it went on and then to bring home the lesson about the wrist the end of the rod was tucked into the sleeve of my shirt and a handkerchief tied around rod and wrist. There was no way I could bend that joint now, although it was beginning to feel as if it was fractured. But slowly, oh so slowly, and joy of joys, the line began to go out in the right direction from rod and reel and no longer wrapped itself around the neck. (The danger of embedding hooks either in pupil or master was obviated by substituting half a pipe cleaner on the line end instead of the usual hook – just as well.) The lesson progressed with three ardent would-be fishermen casting out over the dried grass by now oblivious of the world around them. This was it! Take us to those casting competitions where anglers drop their flies on a penny!

In this other-world ecstacy we were vaguely conscious of a sound from the main road not more than a hundred yards behind us. That metallic sound that means a collision between motor vehicles. And, sure enough, there beside the entrance to the hotel were two cars, their owners in the usual state in such matters. It seems that car number one had slowed to a near halt attracted by the sight of three fishermen casting in the middle of a dried-up field. Car driver number two had seen it too but missed the fact that there was a car in front.

Many hours since that day have been spent pondering on the wording of the insurance claims and the explanatory notes. 'Driving along this narrow road my attention was drawn to three fishermen in the middle of a field . . .'! The casting lesson came to an abrupt end at this point as laughter destroyed all concentration and we thought on what could have gone through the minds of the drivers on seeing apparent madmen fishing in a field. John Sharp came out with the classic comment, 'After all, sir, the water is rather low this year.' I've a feeling the story has been told and retold in the bar the ardent fishermen gather in of an evening after a day on the beats.

The River Barle flows close to the hotel before its confluence with the Exe a short distance downstream, and spending so many happy days down there getting to grips with fishing a memory stirred in my mind. It was a vague memory of words written about the Barle, a distant memory. Recently I came across it again and a couple of sentences say it all: 'Here is a pool by the bank under an ash – a deep green pool inclosed by massive rocks, which the stream has to brim over. The water is green – or is it the ferns, and the moss, and the oaks, and the pale ash reflected? This rock has a purple tint, dotted with moss spots almost black; the green water laps at the purple stone, and there is one place where a thin line of scarlet is visible . . . another stone the spray does not touch has been dried to a bright white by the sun.' The words are Richard Jefferies' from the book of his last essays *Field and Hedgerow*. Looking at it today I can't help but think it shaped my future. That copy is my school prize for English and particularly elocution at Lucton School, Herefordshire. My interest in natural history was already there, and perhaps the imposing elocution lady at Lucton had a part in shaping my voice into something that has stood me in pretty good stead over the years.

Hooked – that's what happened to me, and fishing took on a very important part in my life but I was never destined to be a fisherman of renown because my eyes and ears are always distracted by other happenings around, and without doubt that has been part of the pleasure of fishing. One spot that became a favourite haunt if not hideaway was a series of ponds not far from Dulverton at Bellbrook. This is a dell deep in the countryside approached by narrow country lanes. It's not only secluded, but difficult to find. Where else, for instance, apart from this outskirt of Exmoor, would you have to stop your car suddenly on rounding a bend to allow half a dozen red deer to cross the narrow lane? They stopped as if to say 'who's this invading our territory?' and then clambered up the steep bank on well-worn track to disappear with an expressive flick of their tails.

It was in the same spot in the height of summer that a woodcock flew over in front of me, certainly during the nesting season but no time could be wasted looking for the nest. Never have I found one. Woodcock nests and red deer have something in common – seeing either is a matter of chance, you just have to stumble across them.

Bellbrook is set in a narrow valley with a series of ponds arranged in terraces downstream to the house at the foot of the last, where the spring water supply disappears under the road into a series of deep ponds and thence away. That valley is the place to ease the mind of tormented man, where all the problems of the world are forgotten in the pursuit of fish and the wildlife around. I've always maintained that leisure should be just as organised as one's working life, if not more so. Bellbrook demanded a bag of liquid refreshment, a couple of hours off for lunch and a quiet contemplation of the world around. No matter if fish didn't co-operate in the plan, it was a day for getting away. Much better, of course, if a few rainbow trout were taken as could frequently happen with eight grand fish in the bag. Even one or two would suffice because it gave me so much more.

Here is a spot for the naturalist. One old solitary oak tree beside the ponds would often give sight of a treecreeper climbing its gnarled, wizened bark; ravens would croak and buzzards mew their winged way in the skies above; mallard families explore the edges of the ponds; tawny owls frequently heard in daylight hours; grey wagtails always present, and the silence occasionally shattered by that distinctive whistle of a kingfisher flying up the ponds to alight on a hazel branch and survey the fish that are bigger than he can manage! He'd need to be nearer pelican size to take on some of those rainbows.

Clouded yellow butterflies arrive in this country from their Continental haunts in good summers; some years are better than others and those keen to see them become a bit like the bird-watching 'twitchers' in their anxiety to 'tick'. Try Bellbrook, but you need more patience than usual if you want to take photographs of them; clouded yellows appear in this sun-soaked valley with clockwork regularity.

Travels with natural history programmes have given me sightings denied to other amateur naturalists but one day at Bellbrook came a scene that any producer of wildlife programmes would have given a pension to put on film. Quietly casting away, my attention was drawn to a gentle bow-wave progressing across the main pool. A trout, nose out of the water doing a 'trawl' in reverse? I've seen them doing this, pushing along the breast feather of a mallard floating on the water and maybe it's something akin to 'play'. This though was no fish, this was a snake. A grass snake. I abandoned my rod for a closer look: a grass snake swimming with sinuous movement of the submerged body and only head above the water surface, hence the bow-wave. It was something I'd seen before and is not uncommon for these animals are very capable swimmers. But in the next half-hour four more grass snakes took the same journey in the same direction across the water. Five in thirty minutes.

Getting a really good look was not easy but one of them swam close to the bank giving a close-up view of its aquatic ability, and the grass snake is no slouch in the swimming stakes. What really surprised me was its alertness and survival instinct in what must be its secondary environment. The moment the snake sensed my presence not two yards from me, it submerged completely. Gone was the bow-wave, gone was the swimmer, but in the green tinge of the water it was still visible swimming now with all the vigour of not being last in the survival stakes. That snake stayed under all of five seconds before the snout came out and the bow-wave returned near the far bank. That five of them should be seen within such a short space of time, all making determined efforts to reach the same wooded bank, can only indicate that hibernation time had arrived and winter quarters were their goal. It was the third week in September but if any television producer wants to film such an event he could never have the luck I had. I see from my fishing diary that one of those clouded yellow butterflies was also around that magic autumn day.

The ingenuity of man and the guile of the fish are the factors in the angling equation, although angling itself is not always involved. Using a worm as I have done is not regarded as 'sporting' and some of the present-day lures used to attract trout are anything but 'the done thing'. There are gaudy devices known as 'dog knobblers' consisting of a large hook with a vague head and masses of feathers, perhaps black, yellow or gold. Soft and silky when dry, once immersed the marabou feather becomes waterlogged and the lure is said to resemble the fry of other fish or maybe a large tadpole, depending on the colour. There is no doubt that knobblers are effective but this is supposed to be *fly* fishing and there are any number of artificial flies to choose from without resorting to such devious tactics.

And what about a bicycle wheel that has long since outlived its usefulness as a means of locomotion, a few bits of string and half a dozen bacon rinds suspended to catch a meal from a stream? I've seen it done in Oxfordshire of a summer evening in clear, smooth-running waters where crayfish abound. Crayfish can't resist the bait and frankly I'm not exactly against a dish of crayfish should they be put in front of me!

That Oxfordshire stream is a tributary of the great Thames, and it was on that 'Old Father' that *The Living World* once ventured out to sample the fish population in a stretch near the power station at Didcot where the water from the cooling towers re-enters the river. Scientists wanted to know what effects this slightly warmer water had on the river life, size, numbers and so on. The boat was the property of the Central Electricity Generating Board and with us was the board's fisheries scientist, Terry Langford. It was a well-founded boat but with the additional cargo, beside the crew, of a 240 volt generator with two probes, one dangled over the bows, the other at the end of a long wooden pole held over the stern of the boat. It's always been firmly drummed into my mind that water and electricity shouldn't be mixed: would you use an electric hair-dryer while sitting in the bath? If you do you've led a charmed life! So all this business in the CEGB boat had to my mind the makings of a dangerous pastime, particularly when the generator was switched on and the pole in the stern was waved about in the water. What was happening, of course, was an electric field was being set up around the boat and any fish in that field would be stunned by the shock. But stunned fish, although floating to the surface, recover in a moment and therefore someone needed to stand by with a landing net. I drew the short straw and held the long net pole, desperately concerned not to touch that other pole in the stern carrying one side of the electric current. As the first fish, all coarse fish, came to the surface the fears disappeared and man the hunter took over in the minds of all those scientists and broadcasters in the boat. The 'bag' by the end of the morning included nine different species of which the most spectacular was the pike. There were monsters by the dozen, and some we examined closely in the boat before returning them to the river. The teeth of the pike we saw could have had a chewing-on part in *Jaws* and we were very careful to keep our distance. This electric fishing may sound cruel, pointless and an indulgence, but from the scientific point of view it is the only way that sensible monitoring can be carried out on the Thames. Mind you, what we were doing that day didn't please one chap we saw sitting on the bank under his umbrella surrounded by the paraphenalia of the coarse fisherman. His keep net seemed to be empty yet before his eyes fish galore were giving themselves up to a boatload of chaps who hadn't the vestige of rod or bait among them.

What a contrast between the Thames and the Test, a southern chalk stream which runs full fast and 'gin clear' to quote Ron Holloway, river keeper on a private stretch of that water whom we met in a recent programme. Indeed, in terms of fishing it's probably more expensive than gin for here is a situation where fishing is good, only wild fish are caught in the ways that would have won approval from 'His Grace' and even if you could afford it you would still find a limit imposed as on public water authority reservoirs. In the same way that gamekeepers on pheasant shoots do all they can to protect their charges against any predators, whether mammals with two or four legs, or predatory birds, so it is with a river keeper. It's a difficult job he has to do in that the principal stalker of his charges is that ungainly, long-legged bird, the heron, and although I tried to draw him on the subject he would not divulge, like any good keeper, the ways he used to keep a high stock of fish. I've a pretty good idea, but then good ideas are best kept to oneself.

'Put and take' waters – that is to say lakes and reservoirs regularly stocked by private owners or water authorities – undoubtedly provide many fishermen with hours of pleasure, a well-stocked deep freeze and a wealth of previously unknown friends keen to enquire into your last success and ever on the look-out for a 'brownie' or rainbow for supper. Many dedicated anglers turn up their noses at reservoir fishing, muttering something like 'That isn't fishing. That is just a case of cast and hope. I'd rather pit my wits against the true wild river fish.' Up to a point, of course, they are right for there's something deeply satisfying about making a difficult cast across the river and plonking your fly right on the nose of a trout seen lurking under the overhanging branches of an alder tree. They go home happy even if the fish weigh in at no more than three to the pound, while the reservoir man is on cloud nine with his limit bag of eight fish totalling 20lb. So there are two different schools of thought and, having indulged in both, it seems to me that river fishing may not be as freezer-filling but it does give the angler a closer contact with river life. It gave me, for instance, numerous encounters with those smart river birds with the white waistcoats and flicking tail, the dippers, and – more exciting – the view of a kingfisher whistling upstream to perch on an overhanging bow right opposite me and then diving into the water to come splashing to the surface with breakfast in its bill. There have been vivid television pictures of this, but that is the only time I've seen it happen and for me it's one of the big bonuses of fishing.

Trout are good fighting fish, particularly those of about 2lb in weight; from my experience, with a really heavy rainbow of 6½lb there's no fight in them. Once hooked, they merely seem to wallow and it's usually an easy matter to haul them in. But if there's one fish any angler dreams of hooking it's the king of them all, the salmon.

The courtesy of a day on a beat of the River Exe came my way from Toni Jones, proprietor of the Carnarvon Arms, and this was an invitation no fisherman in his right mind could resist. Even a fat contract for a day's work from an advertising company would have to be considered very carefully if it came in direct conflict with a chance of salmon fishing. Or rather, delicate negotiations would take place on the excuse that granny had died (again) and could the fat contract possibly be met the following day!

Such an expedition needs a bit of preparation. Enquiries about the suitability of my 9ft 6in reservoir carbon trout rod for a salmon (optimism already creeping in) produced an affirmative answer. Then, reloading the line with a leader of greater breaking strain than used for trout and a selection of gaudy salmon flies completed the preparations. It was a glorious September day as the Exe was approached with some trepidation – indeed nervousness, since this was new territory, a new experience.

A few more flies were purchased from Lance Nicholson who gave the warning of the sage 'You won't get a salmon until this evening.' The morning was a complete blank and so, bearing in mind the words of wisdom, the lunch was more than leisurely and it was mid-afternoon before I ventured back to the beat that beckoned. The bag up until six o'clock was four small trout which took large salmon flies and were gently returned to the water, and one onlooker not noticed behind me. In the effort of casting, my fly latched into his tweed jacket. Lucky it hadn't touched him on bare skin or the ears or eyes. This is something I'm always concerned about. Flies are dangerous with their needle sharp hooks and another very good reason for it being the sport of loners.

That there were salmon running or resting in deep pools and in hollows under larger trees was all too evident. The sight and sound of large fish rising in elegant, extravagant exuberance spurs the angler on to try a different fly or another tactic.

Just before 6.45pm came yet another change on the advice of John who'd now joined me, and as we tied on a small black triple (stoat tail is its name for those who want to know) there was yet again that big splash of a fish moving just behind us upstream. It was a point where the river narrows fast on the far bank and funnels into a hole around a large submerged boulder. First cast, nothing. Second, just a shade further into the run and a brief but definite tug on the line. The fish had been pricked and so it would now be wary. Third cast – bang. No doubt this time there was a fish on the line.

I don't remember much about the next half-hour except the concentration of giving the fish enough line for a run but not too much to allow it to get under the far bank and into the roots of the trees – pulling in and playing it – concern about the rod bending into a 'U' shape in the battle between fish and fisherman. I remember sticking the rod into my stomach somewhere near my belly-button and sliding my right hand further up the rod to help in keeping the tip as high as possible and saying to John that a new navel would be needed if this fish didn't soon give up. 'That's the least of your worries at this moment' was his reply.

Half an hour after taking the fly, the salmon was safely netted. Arms ached, stomach sore from the impact of the rod, but there was the fish, a beautiful hen of 9¼lb. It was the first fish caught on the hotel waters that day and a very decent sized one at that, and on returning with some pride and placing it in the entrance hall on the large dish always there for catches, word soon flew around. Several drinks later in the bar and the telling of the tale to those who'd had no success that day, several times over, and it was time to retire – a happy and contented man.

It has long been a source of concern to fishermen and scientists alike why a salmon should take a fly when it is a known fact that it doesn't feed while in fresh water making its way upstream to the spawning grounds, high in the gravel shallows. Boredom? Play? Irritation at the continuous sight of a stupid fly being flicked over its nose? One theory that does hold water, if you'll pardon the pun, is that the fish needs reassurance that it is in the river where it hatched and has to 'taste' the environment at various stages on its journey, just to make sure that its senses have guided it into the right waters.

Having said that, I'm still slightly perplexed about the salmon's starvation diet. This was further compounded on finding on my salmon day a diabolical lure that someone presumably up to no good had lost not many yards from the point where my fish was taken. It was an enormous treble hook with a heavy lead swivel weight. Enclosing the hook was a very large prawn wrapped around by bright red wool. Surely it was the prawn that was meant to tempt the salmon and, if so, for what other reason than food? I rest my case.

The nylon line attached to that strange lure I retrieved was of such strength it would have landed a shark so was obviously not the work of a sportsman, but I sometimes wonder if so-called sportsmen are always as pure as they're painted. In our travels with radio programmes around the country, walking as we often do in watery places, whether river, stream, canal or reservoir, we always pick up for safe disposal any discarded nylon line left behind by thoughtless fishermen, people who apparently don't care that such line entangles the legs of many species of birds and often leads to their death. It's usually the coarse fishermen who take the blame but the anglers for trout and salmon are often no better. Walk around any of the Bristol Water Works waters, Chew Valley, Blagdon, the Barrow Tanks or indeed anywhere that men pay money for the privilege of fishing. The indestructible nylon is everywhere in short lengths or tangled balls, spelling disaster for birds. I've seen a swan with a large length of line round one leg. It would get tighter and tighter until it cuts right into the bone, infection would set in, and the bird would probably die just because a fisherman didn't think, or didn't want to think. So please, fishermen, anglers, call yourself what you will, please try not to leave any nylon line lying around and if you find some that others have discarded pick it up, take it home and destroy it on the bonfire or place it in the rubbish bins that most fisheries provide.

12
THE GARDEN

I had no memory of nodding or winking at an auction nor visiting a stock market, so how did those pigs get in the garden? It was a slightly muted sound – probably due to the efficiency of the double-glazing – but definitely, there, outside the french windows was the snuffling and grunting that sounded like pigs! This is the moment when the ordered mind takes over. No neighbours have pigs; half of them wouldn't put up with the smell anyway. The nearest farm keeping pigs is all of two miles distant. Possible.

They *were* pigs! At least as I gently drew the curtains apart and squinted through the window, the voice of James Robertson-Justice boomed back in my memory. They are hedgepigs, boy, hedgepigs, not hedgehogs! And listening to the noise his description was apt for what I was hearing was a hedgehog jousting match: in other words the old eternal triangle was at work again sorting out male and female, the mate and the mated to be! It's often asked how hedgehogs mate and the snappy answers are either 'with difficulty' or 'carefully', but this preamble was anything but gentle. There were three hogs out there in the garden and it was a case of two males competing for the favours of one female with the initial sounds being the courtship of a single male trying to persuade her to submit. This presumably attracted the other male and that's when the tournament began. They don't exactly gallop at each other with flying banners but their spines are rather like the lances of the jousting knights of old. Not wanting to disturb this intimate moment in their lives, no more lights were switched on nor did I reach for the camera with flash attachment. All this activity must have lasted for half an hour with not much of it very clear, apart from the side-to-side pushing and shoving and the continuous grunting. It was only next morning that the full extent of their tourney came to light with the garden border plants in some broken disarray where the vanquished had been pushed into the floral corner ropes before, presumably, ambling off in search of other amorous pursuits.

This is but one isolated moment of pleasure that these charming mammals have given me in the garden. Year after year, the weekly milk bill has risen in order to provide them with trays of sustenance, but rationing the supply was necessary when the cats from next door found this free addition to their menu.

Some hedgehogs have been quite good posers for the camera, and having two at the food tray became quite common, although stealth was needed in stalking to get into the right camera position. They would never appear on their paving-slab stage if the window was open so all the shots had to be taken through the window glass. Moral: keep the glass clean! Sometimes hedgehog would arrive with unexpected feeding companions, the sort that would have ended up as a hedgehog feast themselves in normal circumstances. The first time these two were seen together at the tray I couldn't believe my eyes for as the hedgehog slurped away noisily at one side of the tray, on the opposite side of the dining table was a large slug, body draped over the edge of the container like a fur round a scrawny neck, anxious to have as much milk as possible. This odd meeting between 'prickles' and 'slimy one' became quite common and my photographic proof caused quite a laugh in the studio on one occasion during a recording of a *Wildlife* questions programme. One of the speakers was going on at some length about the way hedgehogs will grab and eat any slug they came across. The photograph, quietly drawn from my briefcase and handed across the table, collapsed a distinguished zoologist!

They're greedy feeders when they find the nightly supply of milk, putting their front paws into the tray to keep it still as the level of milk falls in direct proportion to the increased rotundity of the stomach. And they visibly and audibly 'burp'.

I am always concerned on seeing small hogs in the garden late in the autumn, for their chances of getting enough fat stored to see them through a cold winter's hibernation are pretty slender. All one can do is supply as much food as possible to help them through. They are creatures I have a lot of time for and they give me untold pleasure observing them in the garden. It's worth a few extra pints on the milk bill, but all the time we feed them they ignore the pesty slugs that they could be more usefully employed controlling. Another case of swings and roundabouts.

Hedgehogs, then, are just about the only mammals seen in the garden, apart from the wandering dogs that use it as a short cut or cats that are never shown the welcome mat. A big boot heaved from the back door is the only greeting they get, and although it's known that if you want to keep neighbourhood cats out of your patch the best way is keep a cat yourself to lay claim to the home territory, pussies and I have never seen eye to eye. They can put on airs and graces suggesting faith and affection but once outside the door they revert rapidly to something akin to their wild cousins! Hence the big boot, particularly when I see one stalking up to the food put out for birds with all the guile and stealth of a tigress. Cats are not for me. Small mammals do use the garden, but I've never seen them, only the clues they've left behind like the cracked shells of hazelnuts fallen from the trees telling me that mice do pay me a call, as does a fox – never seen, only detected by scent!

My garden is really a compromise between giving pleasure in its sights and scents throughout the year while at the same time attracting as much wildlife as possible, thus giving me and them a bonus. It sounds as if a splendid plan was drawn up in the early years, but nothing could be further from the truth. Like Topsy, it just grew and grew as more and more treasures were found a convenient space, some to thrive, others to succumb through being in the wrong place or the wrong climate.

There was a gardener who claimed that she could have a flower for every day of the year and her Somerset garden during her lifetime proved the point – Margery Fish. Indeed, a direct descendant of one of her plants is flowering this January day as I look out of the window. It's not much of a flower in the eyes of some because it's green – and poisonous. The stinking hellebore, *Helleborus foetidus*, of luxuriant growth and with flowers that take on a purple tinge as the season progresses. But in terms of the weather it's as tough as old boots. Hard seed pods form in the late spring and as the summer sun becomes warmer they split and scatter the seeds in considerable numbers. Last year, clearing up around the hellebore, sixteen seedlings, robust and deep rooted came to light.

The beauty and the value of winter-flowering plants and shrubs are appreciated by insects as well as us. Outside the windows, close by the hedgehog feeding station, appropriately is another. I call it *Mahonia japonica*: it's that tough merchant with thick prickly leaves and splendid pendants of yellow flowers with the adorable scent of lily of the valley. Now that really does produce a buzz of activity. It's like giving the bees a Christmas present for it's common on a milder day in December or January to find a dozen bees busy about the bush. There's a double benefit to the mahonia in that blackbirds go for the berries in mid-summer ignoring all else and quickly clearing them, but to keep the shrub within bounds and shape it should be pruned as soon as flowering is over. Therefore the old Jones compromise comes into play and each year it has a partial prune so that some of the berries are left for the birds!

It is astonishing how active bees can be in the winter months when the temperature is but in the mid-forties. (I still believe in good old Fahrenheit and refuse to admit the existence of Celsius!) To give those bees a bit of a bonus, the few heathers in the garden are once again winter-flowering varieties, and long before the first bulbs give spring scent and colour the insects make a bee-line for the ericas. *Daphne mezereum* is another with both scent and sight to gladden the eye and feed the insects.

So winter gives way to warmer days and the promise of new life sensed a few weeks earlier produces birth in vibrant beauty. Crocuses and grape hyacinths are the first to appear and that seems the signal for bumble bees to shake the lethargy of winter quarters from their wings. Some gardeners blame sparrows for clobbering their crocuses, but in my case the culprits are the bumbles! Just watch them bombing about above them, then to settle on the slender, just-open flowers. Weight of bee too great, stem of flower too slender! And that's the end of another crocus. Still, it's spring and there's plenty more to come; the critical days for the insects are over. Although I pride myself on having eyes that see more than most, I have never noticed any insects among that real rural announcer of spring, the snowdrop. Something must visit them, but I've yet to be on the spot at the right time.

It'll come as no surprise that butterflies are catered for in the Jones garden cafeteria: in my case the high-rise Hilton of the catering world is an untidy clump of buddleia bushes. It all started in a small way in a scruffy stunted plant trying to put its roots down between a wall and the tarmac of a BBC carpark! It was gently purloined and given the freedom to spread and express itself and has become, with its offspring, a small buddleia jungle. The Hilton analogy is apt since what we do in providing food plants for insects is giving them a chance to top up their tanks on their fragile way through life. It's all worth it when I look at the dozens of butterflies flitting from flower to flower on a sunny day – anything up to fifty at a time dancing in the sunlight with the frenzy of animated confetti. I counted nineteen different species in one year and that was the year when a humming-bird hawk moth joined in the frenzy – a rare but more than welcome visitor hovering over the flowers just like its avian namesake. Oh for the ability to count its wing beats.

Moths are very much in mind with the summer border plants, and once again it's a compromise between me and them! Two plants that give most satisfaction to both are night-scented stock and nicotiana. Each will last in flower until the first of the late autumn frosts. Each has a glorious evening scent and moths come in hordes when all other insect activity in the garden has ceased. Each to its own place.

One night flier about in numbers in the summer of last year took me back to younger days when a heavy bang at the window gave warning of May bugs. Heavy lumbering beetles that can cause a painful collision should they miss the window and fly into you! The window banging started last summer! Several of them drowned in the water butt; others were found whiling the days away in the close foliage of the rockery. I was reminded of them in the pre-winter clear-out of some of the borders when, gently forking through the soil among the roses, a long, creamy-white larva came to light. It was a fearsome beast about three inches long with a pale orange face and three pairs of legs: the larva of the cockchafer, a new find for the Jones garden.

There is a theory that species distribution maps covering the British Isles with blacked-in five kilometre squares like a patchwork quilt are about as reliable as the opinion polls that politicians cling to or cast aside depending on the way the swingometer is moving! In the case of the maps, the more cynical loudly proclaim that they are more representative of competent observers than the mammals or birds they should record. In other words, some of the white squares could well have been black had blanket coverage been achieved in conducting the survey. It goes without saying that given two black five kilometre squares with one white between them on the same latitude then surely the species in question also occurs in the gap!

Let's apply this theory to the smaller areas of our gardens. Here the number of species seen is a reflection of the time spent observing. I'm convinced that many a garden has a higher number of visitors than the householder has seen. Take a house where everyone is out about their business during office hours. Sightings therefore are confined to the top and tail hours of the day with a great gaping void in between. So who's to tell what calls when you are out? I've proved this time and again in my own locality where the nature of my work gives me long days just looking, whereas the houses around are empty and on enquiring if such and such a bird has been seen in their patch the usual answer is a firm 'no'. But they weren't there as some rarity flipped from one Englishman's castle to another. I would go further. The betting must be that all other things being equal, such as the available food, then the house without the eyes peering out and not a movement of doors or curtains will have an even greater number of species than mine.

I'm satisfied, though, with my little lot and 'little' is really an apt description of the Jones estate. But even a window box can be a miniature reserve, so no matter how big or how small, it may be of use to some humble species if only for a few invertebrates in the soil of the plastic container on the window sill!

Quite obviously, with a couple of wire feeders hanging from a bird table not more than three yards from the kitchen window, the most abundant birds are the tits – the blue, the great and the coal – but then, come a spell of hard weather, a couple of marsh tits use the feeding station. Smart black caps on the head and short 'beard', also black, under the chin. Beware, though, not to confuse it with the willow tit; they're very similar.

Tits apart, all the usual garden birds are there. Greenfinches feed messily on the nuts in the feeders, distributing to the grass as much as they eat to the benefit of birds that haven't learnt the knack of perching on the wire and taking their fill at will, chaffinches being a case in point. One robin has been seen perching on the small crosspoles attached to one of the feeders but robins too stay on the deck and pick up the pieces!

Pied wagtails too 'flick' and scuttle along under the table waiting for the greedy and wasteful ones to drop a few crumbs like the hedge sparrow. (What a much better name is dunnock, for the bird is much smarter and more tuneful than the house sparrow.) What is so good about this method of feeding is that one doesn't have to litter the grass around the table with food for those who can't get it from the feeders. Food on the ground only attracts starlings who seem to have a post of sentries around the village and once a few crusts of bread are thrown out of a window there's a winged and noisy invasion as they descend and grab everything in sight. They're the garden marauders in my book and not my favourite bird, but they are not unattractive. Just take a close look at the myriad colours in the plumage of a starling as the sunlight hits it. It's a sparkling collection of jewellery.

Starlings have caused me to jump out of bed or dash to the garden as they are such marvellous mimics. One day a curlew was heard on the roof! A glance to the roofline revealed one starling in full curlew song! But one occasion I made a mistake. Lying in bed I heard the 'yaffle' of a green woodpecker and dismissed it out of hand as being as impersonating starling rehearsing its act. The sound persisted until I could lie abed no longer and looking out of the bedroom window there on the lawn was indeed a green woodpecker! It was pecking around and had found a supply of ants or their eggs. What made me so glad, the duvet having been thrown aside, was having the close-up of the bird from above. Normally we see it but fleetingly pushed hard against a tree-trunk almost as if it's perching on its tail. My view from altitude showed that the bird also uses that strong tail while on the ground as the third point of balance. It rests on a tripod.

There's one penalty you have to pay in attracting birds in some numbers to the garden. The unfriendly neighbourhood cats soon get to know of the congregation and try to cull a few, but more spectacular and less easy to deal with are the visitations of another bird wont to take a meal from its smaller cousins. You have to be right there at the moment the sparrowhawk strikes for it happens so quickly that blink and you'll have missed it. The only sign will be the sudden dispersal of the survivors into whatever cover they can find! Oft-times this bird of prey isn't seen but the evidence comes to light afterwards in a pile of breast feathers from a blue tit in one corner of the garden where the hawk has plucked its prey before taking the meal.

Butterfly wings, of tortoiseshell, peacock and the whites, littered on the ground around the garage and close to the buddleia forest, set in motion another 'whodunit'. This was a classic case of the mistake of jumping to the obvious conclusions. The answer that stood out a mile centred around the spiders that set their silken traps along the roofline of the garage where patently they enjoy a good catch and a good meal. There's no doubt in my mind that some of the insects fell prey to the spiders for I have freed quite a few from the tangled webs woven to deceive. But the number of wings left lying around suggested something different. There were no more clues to work on until an unlikely bird of prey, perching on the roof of the garage, suddenly fluttered out into the buddleia and picked off a small tortoiseshell butterfly. Not satisfied with that it then took a peacock! This was a juvenile spotted flycatcher and the fact that it was taking peacocks with their warning eye-spots on the wings suggests that the SFC hadn't read the definitive books about 'keep off' markings that many insects sport. With careful observation it soon became clear that it wasn't just one flycatcher reaping the butterfly harvest but a whole family of them.

For reasons I have never fathomed, the garden seems blessed with more colonies of ants per square yard than the average plot possesses. No complaints, for I've never been bothered with them inside the house making an ant-line for the sweetness of the kitchen cupboard as happens in some households. There comes a day in high summer, sometime in late July or early August, when the activity in the colonies becomes frenzied and the sky above is suddenly filled with gulls and jackdaws and house martins and swifts wheeling and swooping. Sparrows and some house martins can be seen along the path edges picking and pecking. This is the mating flight of the ants and a chance for many birds to gorge themselves. In the case of the swifts, I offer a personal theory. It's all connected with the natural cycle of life. Birds time the nesting, laying of eggs and thus hatching of chicks to coincide with the peak of available food supplies peculiar to their own needs when the fledglings need vast quantities. Could it be that the swifts also time their departure from our shores, in August, *after* they've taken on enough fuel to see them through at least part of their long flight to the southern hemisphere? It's certainly a fact in this area that once the nuptial flight of the ants comes to an end the swifts rapidly disappear. It makes evolutionary sense to my non-scientific mind.

The arrival of a 'vagrant', that is a bird from another country on our shores, whether from the Americas or Russia, sends a great twitch through bird-watching circles, so much so that it is not uncommon for them to hire private charter aircraft to fly them from remote parts of Scotland to the Isles of Scilly to join other 'twitchers' pointing telescopes or zoom-lensed cameras at some tiny, insignificant wader or dull warbler. Another tick to add to their list and, for these people, rarity bird-watching is almost a disease. I'm not decrying their efforts for we each have our own hobbies. It's not much different from the golfer who wants to play every course in the country or the fisherman who adds more and more rivers to the notches on his rod.

This enthusiasm is understandable when a stranger turns up in the garden, like the day when on the bird table there was a robin that was wrong. I couldn't take it in for a moment that this almost black bird had changed a red breast for a rufous tail which it continuously flicked. It was indeed a male black redstart, never seen in the garden before, never seen again but those few moments were pure magic: the bonus in the investment of caring for birds.

Of less importance, but none the less surprising, is the bird that escapes from the gilded cage: the blue budgie and the strange canary, still not identified, that came to the table, fed on the nuts and generally caused havoc among the regulars. Someone must have missed it for it had quite a beautiful song given from the top of a tree once it had a full crop!

One day there was what appeared to be a house sparrow, but it had a darker head and a white collar! It makes you look twice when such a stranger appears and the second glance showed that it had been ringed. The next day this male reed bunting was joined by a female, and the pair, as I thought, stayed around the garden for two or three days until looking at the two of them one morning something was wrong. The male had apparently lost the tagging ring from its leg. It was then the penny dropped. My pair of buntings was in fact a trio which was confirmed the next day by seeing all three around the bird table at the same time, two males and one female. This was another 'first' for the Jones bird observatory but not all that surprising since there are small areas of reed beds between the village and the Bristol Channel and certainly the birds nest in these. I can only suppose that they were finding the food more to their liking and easier to come by than that out in the reeds.

Until the past winter, when their calendar must have suffered some aberration, blackcaps would arrive in the week before Christmas and this regular pattern has been followed for ten consecutive years until this year they were three weeks late.

I think Bristol can claim to be the area where it was first noticed that these small smart warblers didn't migrate to warmer climes south of the Mediterranean like the rest of the tribe but stayed and braved our winters. That needs some qualification. It is more likely that the blackcaps seen in southern gardens have indeed made a migration from further north, but instead of going further have found the south quite productive enough to see them through. They also seem to change their eating habits. The mainly insect diet of summer gives way to seeds. From my observations they are quite happy with the small black berries of a garden honeysuckle or buddleia seeds, but having said that it is more than possible that there could be something of their usual insect diet hiding away the winter in the buddleia foliage. It's not insects, though, that attracts them to the mass of fruit on the ornamental crab-apple trees whose roots are in the next door garden but whose branches are mainly in mine! After the first severe frost of the winter these bright red fruits are no longer like bullets, but soft enough for any bird to get at the seeds.

Not only were the blackcaps late in taking advantage of the Jones hospitality this past winter, their behaviour was also out of character. Three in number, two hens and one cock, they have tried food items not tackled in previous years. The cotoneaster berries still seem to be the main standby, especially for the cock bird, but the hens have become so tame that they are wont to sit on convenient perches close to the kitchen window, one on the right-hand side of the garden, the other on the left. From there they

143

make surreptitious flight in a dipping then rising arc for the window sill. I see them take off, apparently diving to the ground and then in a fraction of a second there's the chestnut head bobbing outside not two inches from my nose. I don't know whether I should take this as a compliment to my culinary ability but their favourite food was something lovingly cooked and then found to be a disaster – Welsh girdle cakes, and my first attempt was an abysmal failure. Those that know made helpful suggestions about too much fat in the mixture, too much fat in the iron frying pan. Whatever went wrong, it was right for my blackcaps. They would sit around and wait for the sound of the window opening and now, with a February freeze-up two weeks old, they have cleared me out of Welsh cakes. Another culinary disaster is called for, but one word of warning. Window-sill feeding can lead to collisions between glass and bird! Leave those windows as dirty as possible.

One winter, during a period of particularly bad January weather of snow and frost, the berry-bearing trees that abound along our boundary wall became the noisiest but most exciting habitat I've ever seen in any garden. This was the great invasion of the starving flocks of redwings and fieldfares. These are beautiful members of the thrush family. The redwing is like a song thrush with speckled breast and a long, light-coloured stripe on the head that looks for all the world like an elongated eyebrow! The most distinctive feature, though, is the red plumage under the wings which shows at the most brilliant when the bird takes flight. Nearer mistle thrush in size and markings is the fieldfare, a big bird often congregating with its fellow migrants during their stay on our shores. The colour of blue-grey slate is the hue of the head and rump of this splendid bird.

Once they've cleared the hawthorn berries from the hedgerows, the redwings and fieldfares have to seek pastures new, and I've seen huge flocks of them in fields in the Channel Islands where it's infrequent for a frost to harden the grassland enough to stop a pecking bill penetrating. So these resort to town and country gardens and parks where the trees planted for our pleasure become veritable lifesavers for the thrushes. They are noisy, aggressive among themselves, ever on the move seeking a riper apple, messy feeders dropping as much pulp to the ground as they consume. But this benefits others, often too timid to get involved in the battle in the branches!

There were anything up to fifty redwings and fieldfares on the trees at any one time. (The trees are probably *Malus robusta* but the identification tags have long since rotted away.) Two trees, well laden with fruit, but how long could the thrushes' food supply last? Not more than a week according to my mathematical calculations (a way of describing sheer guesswork).

In a moment of enthusiasm and wishing to pass on my good fortune to others, I suggested to *The Living World* office that they might be interested in a short broadcast from the garden. Nothing happened for two days by which time the fruit on the trees was disappearing as if consumed by a swarm of locusts. By friday, now three days later, things, as they say, started to move! 'We shall broadcast "The Living World" *live* from your house on sunday afternoon' came the laconic message. The apples will never last that long I thought, but what I soon discovered was that other folk in the village had similar trees and every time the flock left me they pushed off round the corner. Then the technical wheels began to turn and the first idea of using the transmitter of Radio Bristol's radio car had to be abandoned when it was discovered that the topography of the house prevented any signal reaching Bristol. Next came the linesmen from British Telecom climbing up poles and opening up mysterious metal junction boxes along the roadside. They were desperately searching for a pair of spare unused telephone lines out of the village and first prognostications were far from encouraging. Yes, a pair of lines had been found, but no, they were not of broadcast quality. And the fruit on the trees was still going fast. By late friday afternoon the Telecom men came to the door beaming. It's all right! You can go ahead.

By now, of course, the village was agog as to what was happening in the High Street and secrecy was called for since the last thing needed on sunday afternoon when we hoped to watch the birds in the garden was a huge congregation of onlookers. Lots of people spell very few birds. And I prayed that the trees would still have fruit when we went on the air!

Only dedicated enthusiasts or the mad would open their houses to a BBC outside broadcast crew when the snow lies thick on the ground. They are as careful as they can be, but cables have to come in, damp, dirty cables bringing snow in their wake, through open windows and doors, along the walls, over the carpets. I was lucky, having been brought up in the business so to speak, and so every available old newspaper found a new use apart from wrapping fish and chips! I littered them everywhere. After lunch on sunday when the producers and secretaries and the rest of the cast had arrived, we went into the hide: the kitchen!

Fortunately, it's a wide kitchen window with room for three of us to perch on stools at the sink and peer out. Peter Ferns had come from South Wales and from the RSPB, John Andrews. We were linked by line to Chris Mead of the British Trust for Ornithology in a distant studio. Come to think of it, had he been in my kitchen with the rest of us the space would have been more than cramped. And yes, the crabs were lasting!

We had bugged the trees: one microphone placed securely on the fencing underneath them. The sounds that microphone picked up before the broadcast began made us all pray it would happen again during *The Living World*. We had one more concern in the back of our minds. The light in late January begins to fade shortly around 4.30pm, the time of the broadcast, so, just in case, we recorded a section about half an hour earlier. A belt and braces approach. We needn't have worried. The light held, the redwings and fieldfares were there in large numbers and other garden birds too, including the blackcaps, put in an appearance. We couldn't have written the scene had we tried, but doing it 'for real' and finding it worked was one of the most satisfying of all my natural history broadcasts.

What was so encouraging about it was the reaction afterwards. It produced far more letters and comments to me than any other broadcast. So many listeners heard the programme and realised they too had redwings and fieldfares in their gardens. They hadn't put names to them before! Others who knew and loved the birds wrote to say how much our experience in the Westcountry had been mirrored in their localities, from Ireland to the Midlands. All very gratifying.

So the broadcast ended and, typical of outside broadcast crews, the dismantling of gear took no time at all. We all sat around on the lounge floor consuming the remains of the Christmas cake, mincepies and sausage rolls and decided it would be appropriate that another fruit of the countryside should provide *us* with sustenance. The Jones sloe gin store took rather a battering that day.

The snow hung on for a few more days until the poor old *Malus robusta* trees were bare and there was the sorrowful sight of the thrushes still arriving looking for food. It was then that local farmers came to my rescue with bags and bags of stored apples going rotten. These thrown out as often as necessary gave the birds yet more food and they stayed in diminishing numbers until the snow went as quickly as it had come. With the thaw so the birds went too and I like to think that my efforts had been useful and that repayment had been made for the pleasure they gave me and countless *Living World* listeners. They did leave behind a legacy. Clearing out the borders later in the year dozens of seedlings came to light where the birds had fed, good healthy seedlings of the *Malus robusta*. After all, the seeds had been dropped covered in fertiliser!

And there was one more to add to the garden list. For a few days the tit feeders were almost 'possessed' by a smart bird with a speckled breast soon identified as a female siskin. It shouldn't have needed confirmation from the books for here was a bird feeding on the nuts upside down, clinging onto the wire mesh. When I thought about it the penny dropped. Siskin would feed like that on alder trees to reach the cones, clinging to the end of a slender branch and reaching down to get at the seed heads.

Paul Nicholas

13
WHERE ON EARTH ARE WE GOING?

The panorama of patchwork that is our countryside today presents a sense of reassurance in that, if only we could see it for ourselves from a spacecraft many miles high, the weirdly shaped fields and pastures, the wetlands, the woods, moors and mountains would look as if they had been there, unchanging, since time unremembered. We know that is not the case. We know that forest used to cover the land and if we need the proof, the sunken forests uncovered at low tides around parts of the coast tell the story: stumps and trunks suspended against decay and the ravages of time, or the timber preserved in bogs and peaty moors.

As for the forests that remain, their origins lie in the hunting rights of kings and their favourite courtiers in the days when the penalties for poaching were gory, and sometimes fatal. And those cosy, compact woodlands on the patchwork quilt of agricultural land, were they too royal preserves? They have only survived because of the shooting interests of landowners who pursued their sport by keeping coppices fit to hold pheasants, and by managing their fields to produce not just a crop of corn or grass, but the additional harvest of game. I would defend shooting in those terms. It is cropping, harvesting, while giving the owner the pleasure of shooting with precision, shooting to kill cleanly, not to wound and allow the target to die in agony. Although there are those who shouldn't be allowed with a pop-gun in their hands, never mind a lethal 12 bore – people who take no pride in being 'good shots' but in merely owning a gun.

The moment for confessions. I owned a gun for many years. The first time I fired one I was but nine: the weapon, a .410; the tutor, my father: the target, a house sparrow's nest in the top of a holly tree. Gamekeepers, though, were always conscious of safety in shooting and the old man was concerned that it is never too early to learn any lesson and the handling of shotguns in particular. You could almost say I was born with the sound of shooting in my ears, and today I will follow a shoot, without a gun, but still applaud 'the good shot'.

If the full confession of a man apparently and publicly devoted to conservation should be needed, I'm happy to confess. I remember the first pheasant to fall to my gun; I remember the last. The first was during wartime days on a brief trip back to those Somerset hills from London. The object of taking out the gun was a rabbit for the pot. The terrier we had then was a past master at finding his way through thick brambles and had a nose for rabbits. He knew the plan and enjoyed the sport. All one had to do was find a long stretch of brambles and push him in one end while wandering to the other to await the rabbits he sniffed out and pushed through their runs. Sitting targets. With ammunition in short supply every shot counted. That terrier had a nose for anything that moved. From his yapping it was clear he had pushed a rabbit out to the flank and my usual ploy wasn't going to produce any bunny for the pot. What he had in fact disturbed was a cock pheasant and the stupid bird took off and flew high over a line of old beech trees right over my head. It was automatic, my swing at the target, and 'bang' down it came which for the .410 was a pretty good shot. There was, of course, the problem of the old man. I went back to the house somewhat sheepishly, expecting the hottest of roastings. 'Ah', he said, before my spluttered explanation could get into full flood, 'Ah, that'll do nicely for lunch on sunday.' The final pheasant was also in his company, legitimately in this case, clearing out cock pheasants at the end of the season. It was late January, and we were walking under a bank in the middle of high alders when our dogs put up another cock. Like the first so the last, an automatic swing and down it came. He was never given to compliments, the old man, but saying 'I hope you're satisfied with that, let's go home', he was being quite generous in praise.

Those are my disclosures. There were many, many other bags between and there are no apologies, but being involved in a shooting background gave me a greater insight into all aspects of wildlife than anything else could have done.

I have qualms, though, about the lead shot peppered around the countryside. Let's do a little calculation. The weight of lead shot in a 12 bore cartridge is often 1⅛oz. Equate this with, say, ten guns on a day's pheasant shooting and let us be generous and suppose that each of them fires off fifty cartridges. That's around 35lb of lead. Let's take it one stage further and suggest that the same equation holds true for the entire season and that ten days' sport would take place. We're now in the realm of 350lb of lead, scattered over the relatively small area of one estate. There's been no hue and cry of lead in woodland or pasture, although there has been about wildfowlers around estuaries, saltings and mudflats where it's been found that swans and ducks take in the pellets of lead in the course of feeding and many are killed by lead poisoning. My calculation for an inland shoot wouldn't be far away from the truth for a busy wildfowling area. But I would still defend man's right to shoot if he wants to. I would just hope the shooting man does not close his eyes to his responsibilities. It's all too easy to throw the blame for the annual death of four thousand swans at the feet of the anglers and the lead shot they use to weight their lines and spill through ice-cold fingers. Their house is being put in order with what is to be hoped will be a voluntary ban on the use of lead. But maybe the day is not far away when it will be illegal for tackle shops to sell lead weights. Even if the law moves in, there will still be a colossal stock of it in fishing bags and who is going to buy substitutes when he still has unused supplies? It will take some years for the slate to be wiped clean, for the years of discarded lead will still show up in dead birds. While this particular problem winds its weary course, perhaps the shooting fraternity should not sit back in complacent self-righteousness but look to their own house while there is still time.

Farmers who are also shooting men are among my closest friends, and while I have sympathy for the problems that face their industry I can't help thinking that they don't really live up to their self-styled titles of guardians of the countryside. The flak has been flying pretty thickly in their direction and not without reason. Their wounds have been self-inflicted in the matter of straw-burning, adding more miles of destroyed hedgerows to those they've already rooted out mechanically to make way for more efficient and better mechanical technology. I've sympathy. If you're in industry you have to find ways of cutting costs and increasing production. Prairie-sized fields and larger machines have achieved both aims. But at what cost? The few hedges they have left now have to be attacked by machines as well, devices that don't cut a hedge but mutilate it. The pieces of timber fly into roads to the danger and discomfort of other users of the highway. The hedge is clipped top and sides and as this treatment continues over the years the base of the boundary becomes so thin and useless that even an aged ram with a bad memory of what a ewe looks like could still find a way through it. Then comes the final blow. It's no longer any use as a hedge, so it's grubbed out and replaced with fencing or else not replaced at all. Fortunately, there are corners of some fields where the multiple-shared ploughs and cultivators and combines cannot move without complicated three-point turns, and nothing delights me more than to find such niches either allowed to return to nature or else planted up as small woodlands or shelters for a pond. It is happening, but is often only done by those with shooting interests which comes right back to my argument that it is the shooting man chasing his prey who does more for the preservation of the countryside than the man who has no such pleasures.

There are other practices less welcome. Silage pits, so necessary for the winter feeding of stock, are often sited with no thought to where any effluent from them will drain. 'Let it run away' is about the only rule and run away it will, following the contours of the land that inevitably leads it into a watercourse. Result, death to much of a river.

The same is true of fertilisers, herbicides and pesticides: all necessary ammunition in the farming fight for survival, but I sometimes wonder if topography is ever considered in their application. From my observation, nitrates are flung out with gay abandon to produce a better bite of grass or better crop of silage without looking over a field with a view to which way the field slopes. No field is as flat as a billiard table – there is usually a fairly discernible tilt – yet the fertiliser is spread as if it will wash into the soil exactly where it falls. Not true. Come a shower of rain and water will find its level. The result is a concentration of the fertiliser on the lowest part of the field and eventually that too, the excess not soaked into the soil, finds its way into a gully, thence to a stream and finally a river. More death and destruction which could be lessened if more thought were given to the way the operation is carried out. It might even be a saving for the farmer too – perhaps he wouldn't need to spend quite so much on producing a better crop. Maybe he would argue that the time taken to survey his land would not be worthwhile, but isn't it worth at least considering?

153

I shall probably lose some of my friends if I carry on in this vein. I cannot leave the subject, though, without one more broadside at their complacency. The day, I hope, will come when there is much more consideration given to the siting and design of farm buildings. National Parks have some control in hyper-sensitive areas, but perhaps the time is not too far distant when harmony with the countryside will be the rule, not the exception, for farming factory units?

The only uniformity in such buildings is generally a coat of corrugated iron. The biggest blight is the rash of tatty shelters surrounding many villages. You only have to have a pony and a bit of grass and you need a horsy shack. Planning permission? No! Just stick it up anywhere in the field to keep the wind and rain off poor dobbin's back. And when the kids grow out of horses, and dobbin has gone to better pastures (or for meat for the local pack of foxhounds), the shack becomes a meeting place for the local hippies until its iron is no longer corrugated and it falls into another heap of rubbish. Yet if we shoved up such a shack as a lean-to on our house we would soon be in trouble with the planning department of the local council. Dare I make one more suggestion? What about a road-fund tax imposed on those who ride our lanes and roads and think they have greater rights than motorists? Yes, I know the arguments — the roads came about to accommodate horses or horses between the shafts, but that doesn't give them unquestioned right of way especially those riders with not enough breeding to say 'thank you' with a friendly wave to a considerate motorist.

Some of the greatest changes in the countryside taking place today owe their origin to our membership of that wasteful and bureaucratic beast, the Common Market, making mountains out of what were barely molehills and floods out of trickles of wine, not to mention enough milk that we might as well have it come out of our taps and bathe in it. Some countries have made enormous gains out of EEC membership. On my last trip to Ireland I was amazed to see that some parts of the country had been turned into a green-pastured Spain with identical haciendas – or rather ranch-houses – standing where not so long ago there was the smallholding where a couple of cows would be milked twice a day and the churn went to the creamery in the shay drawn by the donkey. Today, the shay is nowhere to be seen, replaced by horse-power hidden under the long bonnets of the signs of wealthy farming, the Mercedes or the Volvo. Just now and then the remnant of industrial archaeology remains in the form of the old homestead alongside the new Spanish-style bungalow, but what a change in so short a time.

There's an example of EEC credit – updating antiquated methods and living conditions and taking the industry out of the realms of marginal farming into profitability. But what of Wales? I recently witnessed changes there that have happened in the past couple of years. The county of Powys, I'm told, is not unique in this respect but its glorious folding hillsides have become scarred, criss-crossed with new tracks leading up to higher slopes and old marginal grazing grounds. Tracks constructed from the stone and gravel washed into convenient banks by the turbulence of the winter floods in the river below. There seemed no planning concern about these tracks, fanning out from a farmstead like the strands of silk in a spider's web. Maybe they follow the old routes used since man first put his sheep on the hillside and brought them down for shearing and selling, but surely there are desperate problems. It's not just the blight on the landscape (one can grant that given time the tracks will become colonised by grasses and be less of an eyesore), it's rather what will happen to the hillsides. It will be possible to take machinery higher up and improve the land. More fertilisers, more ploughing, more wash-off into the water systems and one man in his hillside castle, immune and majestic, will be able to look to higher profits. Will he have any thought for lesser life below him in the rivers and streams?

There are parts of the countryside that are endowed with super-protection, the National Parks of England and Wales. One of the smallest of the ten parks is Exmoor, sitting astride the two counties of Somerset and Devon, and it too owes its characteristic patchwork of moorland pasture, heather slopes, plateaus and deep-wooded combes to agricultural activity. It was a Royal Forest until the early 1800s when a large stretch was sold, and John Knight and his family set about taming the forest for agricultural purposes. Their determination, together with the use of steam ploughs, shaped Exmoor to very nearly what it is today.

It has been a National Park for only just over thirty years and in that time what was regarded as a bureaucratic authority has become accepted as something approaching a helpful if not always benevolent ally. No small achievement when we remember that nearly 80 per cent of the 265 square miles that the Park covers is privately owned. Exmoor folk are independent souls and more than most don't take kindly to being told what they can or can't do on or with their land. There are severe restraints on building and building materials, on private housing as well as farming needs and the strongest controls of all on land improvement. Any blot on the landscape, whether a roof on a house or barn out of keeping with the surroundings, or changing moorland heather into grassland is severely controlled. And bearing in mind that Exmoor's narrow roads and lanes came about as sheep droving tracks or wide enough only for horse and wagon, it is not surprising that many a planning application has fallen by the wayside because sufficient access for vehicular traffic is impossible.

My own involvement with the moor has spread over the years, first as a beautifully scenic place to go, a 'getting away from it all' paradise. Then one day there came one of those buff envelopes. The letter bore the seal of the Parliamentary Under Secretary of State for the Department of the Environment. The outcome was a sentence of three years on the moor! Not a bread and water incarceration but as a member of the Exmoor National Park Committee, one of a team of twenty-one whose duty it is to preserve the natural beauty of the Park, make it accessible and enjoyable to visitors and, above all, remember that Exmoor belongs to Exmoor folk. It is theirs to live in and to make a living.

This was a fascinating sentence to serve, an insight into what is in effect a 'mini government'. The arguments during committee meetings are just as noisy as exchanges in the House of Commons, the slanging matches almost actionable, the astute politicians on the team being especially vocal when the press desks are fully occupied! But it works – with success that is reflected in the adoption of some of its decisions in other sensitive areas: management agreements, for instance. This is a scheme whereby if a farmer or tenant wishes to improve moorland and make it more productive, by ploughing for instance, and his application is turned down on the grounds of the amenity value of the landscape, then negotiations get under way to compensate him for leaving the acreage under discussion as it is. The annual payments are based on what profit the land could make at a given rate of stocking and vary from year to year according to market prices. It's reckoned to be fair on both sides, but the bargaining is as hard as any struck at a county market, although I don't think we have ever resorted to retiring to the local and 'spoofing' for the five pence difference that prevented a handshake on the spot. These agreements are the basis of what is coming in some wetlands which do not enjoy the protection of National Park status but are none the less important in wildlife terms.

Management agreements came about after conservation maps had been drawn up for Exmoor, and I shall always remember being thrown in at the deep end on a lengthy survey of the Park looking at sections that were borderline cases. Should they be included in the map where there is a presumption against land improvement or could they conveniently be left outside? For a shy, retiring broadcaster having to argue for or against was daunting. Often tacit agreement or disagreement indicated by a vote was my contribution. Yet since Exmoor National Park Committee published its maps, other National Parks have been directed to follow suit. I wish them luck.

It may sound as if a National Park has money to burn: not so. About a quarter of the budget comes from the ratepayers of Devon and Somerset and the rest from the National Exchequer, in other words, from our taxes. And there is never enough. This was brought home to us in frightening terms when a farm and a parcel of land right in the middle of the Royal Forest came on the market – no smallholding, but a vast area of 2,260 acres. Significantly Warren Farm was one of the Knight family achievements yet here it was apparently up for grabs. It had no electricity supply, although there was a telephone line that meandered round the hillside, into the Exe valley and up the opposite slope to the farmhouse, surrounded by a wind-belt of trees. It was in no great shape as human habitation, but the potential was enormous. Could Arab money come in and send the price sky-high and turn it into who knows what? The land was within the conservation map – at the very heart of it. Even if management agreements could be negotiated, the cost over the years would be prohibitive. The only option then was to buy. Here again political considerations crept in. Wouldn't this sound rather like land nationalisation? There was one even bigger hurdle: there just was not enough money in the kitty and the cost we were thinking of was over half a million pounds.

Negotiations went on for weeks, even lobbying in the House of Lords as well as sounding out government quangos. Eventually, with no hope of government money, it came, in effect from the National Exchequer, from the National Heritage Memorial Fund normally given to spreading its largesse to stately homes and works of art. In fact, this was the first time the Fund had been used to purchase land of national importance and so another first for Exmoor National Park. Eventually, Warren Farm was bought for less than the expected price, just under the half million figure, and the Fund got some of its money back as the farm and the in-bye land were subsequently sold to an Exmoor farmer, which is as it should be. Restraints were placed on the remaining acreage with grazing rights shared with the National Park which thus retains control. It was a hard tussle but, it is to be hoped, in the long run worth it. There to the north of Warren you can stand on the plateau and scan the horizon in every direction and see not a single human being nor a solitary human habitation. If you creep gently toward a slope you may peer quietly over and see in the valley below a small herd of red deer, quietly grazing, oblivious of the watching eyes. That is Exmoor.

Here was a case of conservation on the grand scale but let us not forget that it was only possible because of a large begging bowl and a generous patron, albeit financed by an annual government grant. Undoubtedly, then, there is money for conservation. Of all the organisations devoted to the cause, the Royal Society for the Protection of Birds has the corner. Compared with others they are rolling in it, but it is only due to astute publicity and giving their donors something in return: their films, their merchandise and publications. County Naturalists Trusts are not so lucky, especially one just getting off the ground, and one such was the Avon Wildlife Trust.

Shortly after we came struggling for breath into this world, we were offered a derelict mill – walls structurally sound, roof anything but – a mill alongside a stream that used to turn its wheels. Today, it stands as a monument to the Trust's founders and their determination to think big. Never mind if we haven't got the money was the philosophy, we've got to have that building and the valley behind it. An appeal was launched under the able direction and co-operation of business people with the daunting target of £285,000, to be designated for the mill's restoration and threatened habitats: patches of land that

159

might come on the market that were valuable in wildlife terms. The target still hasn't been reached, quite, but the mill has been restored and is in use as the Trust's showpiece, offering a centre for education and information.

What the Avon Wildlife Trust has done with Willsbridge Mill and other projects has produced envious glances from other County Trusts, as I've discovered in taking our programmes around the country. 'Oh, Avon are you? How do you manage it?' The credit goes to a determined team undaunted by impossibilities. My own contribution is small. My role is strictly public relations; if they want to wheel me out when an event demands it, then I am there. They, the council members, recognise the value of someone in the public eye as a useful cog in their wheel. But I do get qualms at times. National money for conservation is hard to come by unless you're prepared to look around for it. Much of the RSPB income results from wills, from the estates of concerned people. Some County Trusts benefit in the same way, but with Avon, as with Exmoor National Park, alms had to be sought to achieve nationally important measures. What Avon Wildlife Trust did with Willsbridge Mill, though, would not have been feasible without government money, and it came via the indirect route of community programmes, financed by the Manpower Services Commission. Unemployment threw men and women into the desperation of exploring foreign avenues that directed some of them into helping rebuild a derelict mill, fund-raising or fencing a nature reserve. In effect, then, government money *does* reach conservation measures, but by an indirect route. But should something approaching full employment ever return to our country, and the Manpower Services Commission schemes come to an end, what will the County Trusts do then? It will be back to the volunteers with spades and shovels and wellies. And that reminds me – mine still leak.